The W.O.W. Effect

Cortina D. Peters

Copyright © 2020 by Cortina D. Peters, LMHC, CLC

All rights reserved. In accordance with the U.S. Copyright Act of 1976, the scanning, uploading and electronic sharing of any part of the book without the permission of the publisher constitute unlawful piracy and theft of the author's intellectual property. If you would like to use material from the book (other than for review purposes), prior written permission must be obtained by contacting the publisher at admin@iamsherriewalton.com. Reviewers may quote brief passages in reviews.

Walton Publishing House

Houston, Texas

www.iamsherriewalton.com

Printed in the United States of America

Disclaimer: The advice found within may not be suitable for every individual. This work is purchased with the understanding that neither the author nor the publisher, are held responsible for any results. Neither author nor publisher assumes responsibility for errors, omissions or contrary interpretations of the subject matter herein. Any perceived disparagement of an individual or organization is misinterpretation.

Brand and product names mentioned are trademarks that belong solely to their respective owners.

Library of Congress Cataloging-in-Publication Data under ISBN: 978-1-7341214-4-5, herein

DEDICATION

This book is dedicated to my amazing daughter Morgen,

my bonus daughter Aaliyah, and to all the winners out there who are ready to, or are already experiencing, their W.O.W. Effect.

May this journey be one of enlightenment, purpose and overcoming so that the true winner in you can emerge. You owe it to yourself to be great so why would you whine when you can win?

Love, Light & Elevation

~Cortina

In Loving memory of my beautiful cousin Valencia J. Williams.
May your legacy live on forever.

Carolyn Bens & Regina Watson
My angels in heaven

ACKNOWLEDGMENTS

I would first like to thank my mother Kathy Crist and father Derek Crist for loving me unconditionally. You both have always been there for me, even during the times I thought you weren't. Daddy, thank you for unselfishly always putting me first and being one of my biggest supporters next to mom. Every time we speak, you always call me your superstar and remind me of just how amazing I am. Mommy, I want to thank you for always having my back and always being there when I needed you the most. I love you both from the bottom of my heart and I sincerely thank you.

To my daughter Morgen Peters, you are the reason my heart beats. Thank you so much for being patient through this time-consuming process. I know that movie nights and mommy daughter dates were few and far between but know that my love for you, and commitment to you, will never change. I love you my little Pumpkin, Morgie Pie!

To my aunt Jeannetta Gibson, thank you so much for being my live-in nanny, chef, supporter and company. You made sure that the house was noise free and that the girls, and Bailey, were occupied as I journeyed through this process. Your unwavering support and love are truly appreciated.

To my love Dunchy Louis, I want to say thank you for being patient with me throughout this entire process. Thank you for tolerating my absence; understanding of my mood fluctuations; making sure I had what I needed. Thank you for being a listening ear and for always being honest with me, even when I did not want to hear it. You are truly the ying to my yang and, for that, I love you.

Thank you to Dr. Renee Pinder and Maria Freeman for believing in me so long ago. If I've never said it publicly, I want to thank you for taking a chance on me and entrusting me with your vision at the young age of 27. You both provided for me the space necessary for me to grow, both as a woman and as a leader in my profession. Words will never begin to express my sincere gratitude toward you both. Thank you. I love you.

To my publishing and writing coach, Dr. Sherrie Walton, thank you, thank you, thank you. You gave me the tools needed to bring everything inside my heart to life. Even during our initial conversation God was speaking, through you, to me. I am so grateful for you and your obedience to your calling. You have forever changed my life in so many ways. For that, I thank you.

Honorable mentions: My close friends & family

Thank you, God, for blessing me and allowing the thoughts in my mind to flow into the words collected between these pages. You are so very faithful and loving. Thank you for giving me the patience, strength and courage to go through the process of opening and sharing my life with all the winners out there.

PREFACE

What does it mean to W.O.W.? It means winning over whining. For me, it was making a mental transformation in my life that allowed the winner in me to stand up. It was addressing the whiner inside that wanted to appear every time a negative life situation occurred. It was admitting that I was going through life pretending to be someone I was not. It was learning to take responsibility for my own actions and allowing others to be accountable for theirs. My W.O.W. was a process I experienced through my professional, personal and spiritual life, that prompted an awakening in me to want to do, and be, better.

Quite honestly, I was tired of being a slave to the confines of emotional bondage. I felt like a weight was on my chest and I needed to find a way to remove it. I couldn't breathe. Healing, restoration and joy needed to have my permission to enter my life. It wasn't until I made the conscious decision to do the work, that those things were able to flourish in my life.

I'll admit, I was afraid of letting go of the hurt and pain because it had been a part of me, and my story, for so long. Inviting in something new, something that would change me, was foreign. In spite of my fears, it was time to begin the process of elevating. There was a winner in me she just needed to be discovered.

I was finally able to understand that if I wanted to go higher, I would have to make some very necessary changes, face everything that had damaged me, and make peace with things that had caused me pain. I was committed to discovering the real winner inside.

It didn't happen overnight. It was not easy for me to face feelings of hurt, pain, guilt and shame. With every life lesson learned, more of my confidence was built and I was willing to bare it all. Even if it meant changing the course of my plans, I was ready to do it. I promised myself that I would never allow anyone to destroy, or diminish, the hard work put in to making sure that I became, and stayed, a winner.

The journey outlined in this guide is precisely the path that helped me to create and develop into the winner you see today. My personal experiences, along with my professional knowledge, have helped me to create a road map for people who desire, and deserve, to win.

This victory will not simply be given to you. There are things you will have to do to discover the winner inside. Sometimes in life, something miraculous happens that forever changes the course of our path, for the better. This is what happened to me. There was an aha! moment and the light finally came on. There was so much time wasted hiding the real me that I'd forgotten who Cortina was created to become.

Although we may not fully understand what's happening to us mid-transformation realization of self is necessary to help propel us forward. Learning hard, sometimes painful, lessons has been the highlight of my life. After reading this guide, I hope you too will be inspired to live a life free of fear and full of winning.

Today I want you to begin to see yourself as a winner and face every situation with a winning mindset. Trust and believe that better is coming, and that you are deserving of every great thing that will happen in your life. The principles outlined in the pages of this book will be vital to your development as a winner. Be kind to yourself. Be patient enough to trust the process.

Lastly remember this, even in your darkest times God will always be a beacon of light. My faith has always carried me, even past my book knowledge and work experience. This is the core of who I am. May your winning journey be one of adventure and elevation, even if you have a fear of heights.

Introduction

Hey you! Yes you, the one reading this book. Do me a favor and ask yourself this question, 'Am I a winner or a whiner?' You probably answered, I'm a winner, with a slight neck roll and attitude. 'Who does she think she is asking me this question?' You ask, 'Does she not know who I am?'. Well you're right. You are a winner, but consider the question more carefully. It's much more than meets the eye. Winning requires more than words to make it so.

I would like to welcome you to your firsthand experience with The W.O.W. Effect. As a licensed mental health counselor and life coach my experience in the field of mental health is multi-layered. I have worked in various facilities on the corporate and not-for-profit sides of the mental health profession. I've run large corporate facilities, managing hundreds of employees. I've also been a director at small private centers leading a small team. I've worked with children, adults, geriatrics and special populations such as individuals living with HIV/AIDS, people with eating disorders and the LGBTQ+ community.

For a very long time there was a disconnect between the messages I was giving to my patients and the messages I was listening to about myself. I would witness how the tools I offered brought transformation to my patients' lives, but I failed to perform the very same maintenance in my own life. Even with my vast experience there I was questioning myself about who I was, as an individual.

One day a light bulb went off, causing me to reevaluate how I was living my life, carrying my pains and perceived failures. I decided to refocus my energy and do the work necessary to reshape my self view. I was accustomed to everyone else telling me how wonderful and strong I was, I wanted to be able to see myself in that same light. I had no idea that it would challenge everything in me to get me there. I found myself revisiting places and time in my life that I thought I'd never see again. I became my own patient, and a product of the work necessary for change.

Continuing to embrace my own healing, I reflected on the steps I had applied, and how valuable they were for my transformation. These methods have been compiled and shared in this guide, using examples from my personal life struggles and victories. My desire is for these lessons to help you avoid some of the things I experienced as a result of not having a guide to assist me. My professional training, along with my life experience, was the perfect marriage that helped to manifest this book.

Winning is being able to overcome any challenge, fear, obstacle, defeat, negative emotion or barrier preventing you from being able to walk in your true purpose or become your authentic self. It's being able to rid yourself of the fear or judgment of others; it's not being afraid to stand in your truth. Winning encompasses your ability to see yourself, as imperfect as you may be, as perfectly flawed. It is the ability to believe in your dreams and abilities. It is accepting the power to create your destiny. It is not being afraid to ask for help when needed and being able to get back up after falling. It is going after what you want and not allowing anyone, or anything, to hold you back. Lastly, winning is the ability to love all of yourself for who you are. This is my definition of winning.

I titled this guide The W.O.W. Effect because of the power it possesses. It indicates that you have done something that has caused an effect to take place. The something you did changed your situation, thought process or circumstance. When you say W.O.W. it is a declaration that you have overcome. You can overcome anything. Maybe you've finally been able to make a decision and stand by it, don't take that win lightly. By taking this small step in the right direction you've overcome indecisiveness. Or, maybe you've overcome a challenge and are now standing in your W.O.W., learning how to take the road of a winner. That's also a win.

As you continue to read, think about your W.O.W. and what your W.O.W. experiences will mean to you when you learn to win over whining. The principles you will read are going to teach you how to find and discover your personal W.O.W. Effect and understand what that looks like for you. For the purposes of this book, when I refer to the word E.F.F.E.C.T. I am referring to the E.F.F.E.C.T. model. In your E.F.F.E.C.T. a shift takes place. Something helps to move you from one place in your life to another.

The E.F.F.E.C.T. model, as we will explore throughout this guide will detail exactly what that shift should look like. For now, know that in order for that shift to happen you will have to do the following:

(E)= Evaluate and Elevate

(F)= Face Your Fears

(F)= Focus on the Future

(E)=Eliminate Your Excuses

(C)=Consider the Consequences

(T)=Trust God's Timing

Implementing these steps in your life will help you refocus and clarify the winner in you.

Contents

Dedication iii

Acknowledgments iv

Preface vi

Introduction ix

Chapter 1 : The Mindset of a Winner 1

Chapter 2 : The E.F.F.E.C.T. Model 13

Chapter 3 : Winning Is A Choice 35

Chapter 4 : Getting to the Root of the Issue: Doing the Work 47

Chapter 5 : Winners are Honest: Live Out Your Truths 61

Chapter 6 : Removing the Masks 75

Chapter 7 : I'm a Survivor 89

Chapter 8 : Learning to Let Go and Allowing God to Have Full Control 107

Chapter 9 : Overcoming: The Rebirthing of a Winner 119

Chapter 10 : The Superhero vs. The Villain Within 133

Chapter 11 : Setting Goals and Crushing Them 145

Chapter 12 : The Winner Evolution 165

Chapter 13 : The Power to Seek Out, Access and Ask for Help 179

Chapter 14 : The Victory Lap 193

About the Author 202

CHAPTER 1

THE MINDSET OF A WINNER

"The winners in life think constantly in terms of "I can, I will and I am." Losers, on the other hand, concentrate their waking thoughts on what they should have or would have done, or what they can't do."

– Dennis Waitley, Motivational Speaker

You are entering the mind of a bubbly, outgoing, overachieving woman. Some of the stories and concepts you will have access to will help you understand how I became a winner. When my journey began, I had no idea what I was doing. Have you ever searched for something but weren't quite sure what that something was? That was my story.

I was a professional woman tired of being, and living life, on auto-pilot. I was emotionless, exhausted and without clarity. Like clockwork I engaged in a daily routine: wake up, drive to work, return exhausted, shower and prepare for bed. My career was draining. After juggling a failing marriage, single motherhood and battling cancer, I was done. I had given every ounce of hope and inspiration to my family and my patients. I thought I was strong enough to bottle it up and hold it together. My routine left little time for self-care or processing my experiences. I was programmed to be okay, not to show emotions or reveal my true feelings and, often, went about my days as if everything was fine. It was all a facade.

Growing up I was surrounded by strong women who taught me to take the punches that life brings, and suck up the tears because they were a sign of weakness. Unbeknownst, to me I had become someone I no longer recognized, hyper-focused on appearing to be a winner, not willing to deal with the little girl that was whining inside. It was a hard pill to swallow for a therapist but I had to admit, I needed help!

I desperately wanted to learn how to live a more intentional and purposeful life. In order to do that I would need to forget about everything I had ever learned on how to shield and protect myself from potential and/or perceived hurts. Transparency, vulnerability and trust would need to take their rightful place in my life. I knew it wouldn't be easy, but I wanted to be free.

I was empty, broken, confused and full of sadness when I began my self-discovery. The old Cortina was so used to pleasing others that she didn't know how to listen to her own feelings. She had no radar pinpointing what made her happy. She didn't know how to listen to her inner voice. She didn't understand that winning was less about the outside accolades and more about the inner victories.

The journey to becoming a winner has been an adventurous rollercoaster I still ride even today. Despite the work it required, it was well worth the energy. I am emotionally, mentally and spiritually in the best place I've been in, in my entire life. Anyone who wants to win must do the work. If you want to become a winner, follow along as I outline the steps to discovering the winner inside.

Operating with a winning mindset requires:

Honest introspection: At your core you must honestly assess where the winner in you can be found.

Clarity: You must define, in your own terms, what winning looks like in your life.

Living a Winning Lifestyle: Winning is not a one-time event, it's something you do every day. It's embedded in your winning DNA.

Your state of mind is essential to the process. When you are a winner, you apply winning concepts to every area of your life. It's how you talk with authority; how you walk with confidence; how you think with a winning mindset. Being a winner is not a special occasions visit, it is a consistent part of your life.

Knowing Yourself: Know who you are and do the work so you are able to operate as a winner.

Doing whatever it takes: Proceeding in the mindset of a winner requires you to do whatever it takes to overcome obstacles, believe in yourself, heal yourself and move forward in life, no matter what comes your way.

When you think of a winner, terms like champ, victor or endurance may come to mind. You don't wake up one day and suddenly you have a winning mindset. A winning mindset takes time and practice. There are a lot of things people with a winning mindset endure. Becoming a winner won't be easy. You will have to dedicate energy into caring for the winner you want to become.

The Guide to Winning

This guide is going to teach you the process of becoming a winner through examples from my personal journey. Developing the mindset of a winner is a journey. Before you say, 'Oh no, not another stupid self-help guide,' go ahead and ask yourself why not? Why wouldn't you invest in your better self? What do you have to lose by taking a few moments to read the words on this page and the pages to follow? Oftentimes fear of truth is what prevents people from taking on the challenge of self-discovery.

Self-discovery is healthy. It helps you uncover the areas in your life where additional work needs to be done. Once you outline the work needed, do the work. Fix the areas in your life that need to be improved. If you take this opportunity, the one this guide is presenting to you, then you are on your way to becoming a winner.

Just think of me as your girlfriend, giving you life advice you didn't ask for because she knows you need it. Friends help us see in ourselves, help us recognize what our egos allow us to ignore. You may be saying, 'I know I'm a winner, so I don't need your confirmation. There's nothing here for me.' If you turn the page you might be surprised by the things you'll discover.

It's okay to not always have it together. I've worked hard to peel back the layers that protected me from facing my real self. I was willing to sacrifice my existence for the sake of saving face. I know what it is like to feel alone, like no one understands, or is sensitive to, the things you are going through. I've had my fair share of challenges and disappointments.

It was only after being honest with myself that I was able to become a winner, not just someone embracing small victories as if they were a winner's medal.

Let me share with you a glimpse into some of the things that will be unpacked in the pages of this guide. I've been divorced. I've been involved in domestic violent situations. I was a cutter growing up. I've been molested. I've been assaulted. I've contemplated suicide. I've hated myself. I've felt like I wasn't enough. I've battled cancer, twice. I almost died. I've had my heart broken. I'm a single parent. I've been unemployed. Because I've endured all these experiences, I became a winner who was able to overcome the challenges thrown in my path. You can, and will, do the same.

Life isn't easy; it can be exceptionally hard at times. But even knowing that, winners persevere. No matter how hard it may be, they keep moving through to the good. Just because you are a winner doesn't mean life will be a cakewalk. Trials will come your way. You will need to make a commitment to yourself that you will stick it out through your process. A winner knows tough situations are only temporary. They don't get stuck focusing on what it looks like at that moment and they are free to, instead, focus on life after crisis.

I'm going to walk you around the many barriers that come with learning how to develop a winning mindset. You will be asked to evaluate yourself and take a winner inventory of where you are in your journey. This guide is not just a reader it will require your participation. You'll be asked to reflect, to write out your goals and create a plan for operating in a winner's mindset. In other words, you will participate in, and create your own path to, winning.

Are you ready for this journey? This *is* a journey so settle in for the ride. Journeys, unlike trips, are benchmarked with milestones as well as memories. You will get as much out of it as you put into it so first choose to embrace the journey. You will have to be willing to apply the knowledge; I am merely providing the structure.

Go ahead and see yourself progressing through the pages of this guide. Know that I am rooting for you. You have the power to become, and stay, a winner. Having a winning mindset isn't just a destination. You must put forth the effort and work at it every day. A winning mindset is something that requires daily maintenance. It is up to you to keep exercising the winner in you. Your winning mindset will be tested and challenged. Rise to these occasions when they are presented. They keep that winning mindset sharp and intact.

One of the hardest things about developing a winning mindset is constantly reminding yourself why you can't give up. The simple answer is there is too much at stake for you to think about giving up. Giving up is not a viable option. Begin to say that to yourself every day. Take it in like the medicine it is. Apathy is the infection, this is the cure. Repeat after me, *GIVING UP IS NOT AN OPTION*. Even if you don't believe it now, say it often enough and it will become your reality.

There have been many times in my life where I could have given up but something inside of me wouldn't allow it. Once I realized that everything that was meant to destroy me had no place in my life, once I discovered my true inner strength, I knew that giving up wasn't an option. That allowed me to start living like it wasn't either.

Life is unpredictable and it moves at a fast pace. You must learn to be patient with yourself and expect the unexpected while continuing to move forward. You should not put a time limitation, or expectation, on developing your winning mindset. You shouldn't compare your process to mine. I can't say it takes one month or five years to develop. Everyone's story is different. The time it will take you to develop and stay operating in that mindset is different from anyone else's. What I can tell you is the sooner, and more regularly, you practice the steps the shorter the journey becomes both intellectually and in real time. Action is the great time balancer.

It is easy to become discouraged. Don't give up. As you begin to embrace your winner be careful not to allow fear to creep in. It is very scary to give up the mindset of fear. It will be scary to go from something comfortable to something foreign. New and charge are action words for fear. The way you view your life, and your future, are the reasons fear will be silenced. Are you ready to go on this journey? Embarking on this winning journey is a huge risk. You need to be willing to take this risk in order to develop a winning mindset. For those of you okay with where you are, by the end of this guide, hopefully you will recognize you have already begun to change.

Winner vs. Whiner

Whiners give up and allow their current circumstances to throw them off track. They lose focus. They play the victim and stop taking chances. They might even expect for others to come rescue them, making excuses for why they can't get back up and try again.

The winner sees misfortune as a teachable moment. They take the opportunity to learn and become better. The winner gets back up. They don't stay down or get stuck in the negative mindset. The winner fights through, no matter how hard, dirty, tough or rough it may become. You can't be negative and be a true winner. The winner knows that every situation won't be a breeze, no matter what, they are strong enough to endure.

This guide will ask you a lot of questions. This is because I want you to assess the things holding you back from being a winner in every area of your life. Look at where you are and where you want to go. Do you know what needs to be done in order to overcome and win? I am going to say this, dozens of times throughout the guide, this journey is not easy, but it for darn sure will be worth it. Keep going. Take a chance on yourself. You have more potential inside than you yet know how to harness. You are stronger than you feel. You possess a warrior spirit and have overcome so much to be where you are today. Give yourself a turn. Become a true winner.

You control the narrative of your life. Your thoughts, actions and behaviors dictate what happens next. Winners don't just become winners by saying they are winners. Winners put actions behind their beliefs. Don't allow what people think of you to dictate how you view yourself. Sometimes we allow our past, or what people say, to stop our growth. I'm here to encourage you to stay the course. Keep moving forward and keep your eyes fixed on your goal.

As you read, apply the concepts and strategies presented through the filter of your own experiences. This will help you to make connections and parallels in your life that have previously gone unnoticed. Buckle up and enjoy the ride. You have been granted permission to deep dive into the making, and life, of a winner.

Below are chapter summary questions for you to answer.

What is your definition of winning?

___

What are the current areas of your life that display there is a winner in you?

___

What is the current narrative of your life and how do you view yourself when it comes to being a winner?

___

List any reservations or fears you may have as you prepare to take this journey to discovering the winner in you.

___

What does winning look like to you? What would need to happen in order for you to see yourself as a winner?

___

What 5 things does operating in a winning mindset require?

_____
_____
_____
_____
_____

Chapter 2

The E.F.F.E.C.T. Model

Lucky people get opportunities; brave people create opportunities; and winners are those that convert problems into opportunities.

~Anonymous

In January 2006 I met the man that would become my husband and the father to my daughter. I was in a peculiar place in my life and really wanted to start a family and become a mother. This was something I hadn't ever desired before but the previous year of my life was chaotic and uncertain. I wanted to create a sense of joy and love for myself after everything I was going through with my cancer. I was still receiving radiation treatments and had just called off my engagement to my fiancé and I needed something good to happen to me...*quickly*. My soon to be husband wasn't the type I would usually fall for, but I have to admit I fell head over heels for him not long after we'd met. He was easy going and funny and filled the void that I was experiencing.

To be honest, we didn't give ourselves much time to get to know one another. Within the year we were married and having a baby. I was experiencing a roller coaster of emotions. My life began to change swiftly. With our union, new challenges arose, but the problems didn't start arising until I was about eight months pregnant. I started to see alarming signs that made me question whether I had made the right decision. His bouts of anger would come and go and, over time, they became progressively more intense.

One day I was sitting in our living room talking on the phone with one of my girlfriends. He seemed to think I wasn't paying him enough attention, so he came over to me, snatched the flip phone out of my hand and broke it in half. I was in shock. I immediately yelled, 'Oh you're going to buy me a new phone.' I remember being so mad. I figured that was just an isolated incident. Little did I know that was only the beginning.

No other major incidents occurred until March of 2007, when my friend Asheli and I was getting ready to go to spring bling to celebrate for Spring Break. She had arrived just as I had finished getting dressed. My husband at the time, did not agree with me going and was trying to physically prevent me from leaving the house. He wanted me to stay home. To keep me from going out he ripped my brand new shirt off my body. I was so embarrassed I didn't even want to go anymore. The shame was so hard to deal with that I could not even face her. I was thinking to myself, *What is she going to think? What is happening here? Will this expose what is really going on?* This was not the first time I had felt as though he was trying to intimidate and isolate me, but I was still in denial and disbelief about my reality.

In July of the same year, after we returned from a birthday party, I told him how upset I was about his talking with a particular woman at the party. We discussed the incident sitting in the car in front of our home. Suddenly he pulled out his gun, placed it on the dashboard of the car, and proceeded to threaten me. I didn't know what to do. I was afraid to go into the house with him. I couldn't believe it was happening. I was so scared. I was afraid for my life. He went inside and I told him I needed a minute alone. I franticly called his mother and explained what had happened. She was the only person I felt I could share this information with who would not be biased and non-judgmental.

I escaped his wrath that night, but the abuse continued. There were so many times that he forced me to have sex against my will and I would just cry the entire time. When I told him it was rape, he responded, 'A man can't rape his own wife.' He often physically abused me. I was punched. I was strangled. Not only was I physically and sexually abused but I was emotionally abused by him throughout the course of our marriage. I was so ashamed that I hid the bruises. Those that were closest to me suspected the abuse, but I never spoke up. I tried to keep it to myself. Eventually I did confide in my best friend at the time, La'Rhea. I never openly spoke about the extent of the abuse; however, I know it was possibly suspected.

As a little girl I conditioned myself to withhold my feelings. As an adult I was still holding onto secrets, too afraid to speak up for myself. I didn't see myself as an abused woman in a domestic situation. I would feed myself lies like, *It's not like it's happening everyday,* to deal with the trauma. I distanced myself from other women going through the same thing, but when I heard people talk about women in domestic violent situations as weak-minded and dumb, I would get offended. I knew I was neither but I was abused.

On the outside I appeared to be a winner. I was earning good money and finishing my master's degree. I seemed self-assured, as if nothing could stop me. But inwardly I lived in fear. I can remember telling La'Rhea, 'If anything happens to me, I didn't commit suicide or leave.'

My startle response was very sensitive. I walked on eggshells. It wasn't until I became a therapist that I was able to connect my hyper-vigilance, and my sensitive startle response, to the fact that I was suffering from PTSD. Every time he walked in the house, I would jump. When my phone would ring, or when doors would slam I was on the edge, feeling how I felt every time I thought he was about to put his hands on me.

I compartmentalized my life. I ignored the chaos and abuse going on in my own home. That compartmentalization drove me to excel in my work performance. This was a theme in my life. It started when I was a little girl and it constantly reappeared. When I was sexually molested by my stepfather, I became more involved in school and excelled in other areas. I didn't get the help I needed back then- I buried it. Never dealing with or confronting the person that cause me harm. Never processing my emotional pain or the trauma their actions caused me.

After the abusive occurrences in my marriage, I still stayed because I didn't want another failure in my life. I didn't want a failed marriage that would somehow reflect how others saw me, so I kept up the facade. Then one day, I finally had a breaking point and it caused me to evaluate my life and marriage. I was in the bathroom getting dressed and I casually mentioned to my husband that I needed him to stay home and watch our daughter while I went out. He became aggressive and began to choke me in front of her. At the time she was about three years old and she began crying. I remember thinking, *I never want my daughter to see anything like this ever again.* After that night, any time she would see me crying she would begin to cry and hold me. As a parent I knew I had a responsibility to her. I had to be mindful of how what I was experiencing could affect and traumatize her. The next day I told him that I would not be renewing the lease and that he would need to find someplace to live. We attempted to make it work later, and although the physical violence wasn't there, there were still unhealthy behaviors present.

After evaluating my experiences with the abuse, trauma and miscarrying twins, finally I decided to end my marriage. I asked God to show me what to do and prayed for the strength to do what was needed. On October 8th, 2010, I came home, and his belongings were gone. I felt a sense of relief, as though I could begin to breathe again. I was at a point in my life where I was beginning to grow. I processed some of the unfortunate circumstances in my life but there were plenty more I was actively ignoring.

As you read my story I don't want you to consider me a victim. I tell you my story because I want you to know that I not only talk about being a winner, I walk the winning lifestyle. As I healed, I had to admit to and face the truth of the underlying issues in my life, those that caused me to stay in an abusive relationship when everything inside of me screamed run! I am blessed that I made it out of that situation alive and from there I started working on bettering myself.

The Making of a Winner

The making of a winner is a subtle process. It is important to be patient as you go through the transformation. When preparing to embark on your winning journey, understand that there are actual rules, guidelines, and a road map that you will need to follow. Becoming a winner takes continued effort and reassessment. The first part of that assessment comes when you incorporate the E.F.F.E.C.T. Model into your life. The word E.F.F.E.C.T. in The W.O.W. Effect means that there is a step-by-step method to developing the winner in you. Winners, and aspiring winners, understand the importance of doing the steps in all circumstances.

The E.F.F.E.C.T. Model

(E) = Evaluate and elevate

"We should always be ready to explore our positive and negative traits by evaluating our real self from time to time."— Dr. Prem Jagyasi

The first step in this model is to evaluate your situation. You evaluate so that you can elevate. Evaluating where you are is an essential part of knowing where you need to go. The word evaluate means to judge, or determine, the worth of something. If you don't take time to evaluate yourself, how can you make necessary adjustments? How can you correct things if you don't know what areas need to be fixed? Knowing where you are will help you determine the best course for moving forward. Evaluating helps you determine how to execute your plan. Having a plan will help you end up exactly where you want to be.

During my abusive marriage I had to evaluate who I was and in what direction I was headed. I had to evaluate the danger I was putting myself, and my daughter in. It was no longer a safe situation for us and I had to make a serious choice. It isn't always easy to evaluate where we are, or who we are, because it forces us to look at things we've done, the choices we've made, and recognize our own role in how we've come to be where we are. I had to evaluate how my lack of judgment, and impatience, allowed me to end up married to a man I hardly knew.

Evaluation of self is so important, and an equally necessary part of the process. By evaluating your goals, you are able to determine how your current position aligns with the vision you have for your life. Do you want to elevate in your life? If so, you'll need to evaluate everything connected to you, and do it on a regular basis. Everything that is a part of your journey or could potentially get in the way of you becoming a winner, will need to be examined, observed and scrutinized to see if it is something that needs to be adjusted. This will help you to maintain your focus as you move forward. Winning requires us to rise above our feelings, evaluate and make necessary changes. Oftentimes, we don't want to evaluate because we don't want to do the work that it takes to keep us moving forward.

The Winner

The winner operates with a winning mentality. The winner is self-assured and takes the time to evaluate their progress. The winner has full confidence and has done the work needed to explore and process changes while maintaining a routine to keep themselves from sliding back into learned behaviors. The winner keeps going, without giving up, because they now understand, when you engage with life you win, no matter the circumstantial outcomes. The winner is able to evaluate and adjust when necessary. The winner has stopped making excuses and no longer blames others for misfortunes or unfortunate outcomes. The winner can share their stories of overcoming. Winners have a network of other winners they can work with to ensure each keeps winning.

Go Higher

The higher you climb; the less people will be at the top to meet you. Winners have a deep understanding of the fact that you don't win by stepping on other people, that's a pig pile. Winners motivate, inspire and challenge new winners. In doing so they literally build mountains, pulling as many people as they can up the path. Each person, at every level, can act as hooks and anchors for one another. If you see someone slipping, you'll have built the foundation to help them back to the top because no one likes being alone. You need people to share the view.

Time to Elevate

Once you've evaluated, then you will be able to elevate. Elevating means to raise to a higher place position, rank, or office. Elevating is important. For a very long time I didn't want to evaluate or elevate because I was complacent. If you want to win and operate with a winning mindset you can't be lazy. You must do the work to keep and sustain the winning momentum. Elevate your faith, elevate your effort, elevate your motivation, elevate your expectations, and you will raise everything around you to a higher standard. In order to operate in a winning mindset, everything around you must rise above where it is today. Remember to evaluate and elevate, and in the words of Ciara (the musical artist), 'Level up.'

(F) = Face Your Fears

"Each of us must confront our own fears, must come face to face with them. How we handle our fears will determine where we go with the rest of our lives. To experience adventure or to be limited by the fear of it. "--Judy Blume Tiger Eyes

You must learn to face your fears. When you begin to face the things that cause you to feel a sense of anxiety or angst it may become a bit uncomfortable for you. We often run from, or simply ignore, those instincts. If you do not face your issues head on, they will continue to show up in your life. Being able to set aside your reservations and tackle the things causing you to remain where it is safe, is going to be the determining factor regarding your ability to go further than you would go if you allowed fear to stop you.

How do you see yourself? Having clarity of who you are and what you want is essential. You must see yourself moving from a place of fear to standing in a place of faith. Fear can act as such a strong barrier in your life. You must be willing to scale the wall if you truly want to win and operate with a winning mindset. For a long time I was afraid of failing people, of the unknowns, and of not being good enough. These fears kept me stuck in a place where there was no movement in my life. I often used the horrible moments of my past as a barrier to sharing my true fears.

Growing up, I can remember being very unhappy. A lot of darkness happened to me between the ages of 8 – 13. I didn't feel good inside, I was sad a lot of the time too but no one ever knew it. I often felt like the black sheep and like I just didn't fit in. To others I always seemed happy because I hid the pain so well.

When my mom was in nursing school, we would go over to her friend's house so they could study together with a group. I loved going over to the house because her daughters had the best toys. They had turned their garage into a playroom and we would spend what seemed like hours in there playing. Because they became good friends, my Mom and I were invited to visit their church. Being raised in a Christian home, visiting a friend's church wasn't anything foreign. Like always my mom gladly accepted the invitation and we joined them for their church service. On the side of their main church was a cabin-like building where they would allow the children and teens to go play and have their own religious services. This was back in the 80s, supervision was more relaxed and people were more trusting.

On the night we attended that church service, my earliest memory of being violated occurred. While in the cabin an older boy, who had to be between the age of 14-17 started harassing me. I didn't know what to do. I was so young. I remember feeling very uncomfortable. I wished he would leave me alone. There was a bed in the main area and, after bothering and taunting me for a while, he pushed me on the bed and got on top of me. He would not get up. I begged him to get off me, but he wouldn't stop grinding on me and trying to touch my private parts. There was a teenage female also in the room. she watched the entire ordeal happen without intervening or going to get help. That was very hurtful. I felt so dirty. Even though there was no genital contact or penetration, the violation, level of hurt and intense fear I felt was indescribable.

I left that night with a new understanding of fear. It changed my view of the world. I never told anyone about that night, I kept it to myself. There was a sense of shame and guilt, as if somehow it was my fault. After that incident occurred, I remember crying and feeling unsafe around men and boys. These feelings would only be compounded by other events later in life. This became a mask that I hid behind for years, pretending that I was perfectly fine when in fact I was traumatized.

It wasn't until I was speaking to one of my mentors that I realized I had mastered the art of pretend. I never dealt with the fear from the situation. That fear turned into mistrust and I hid it from everyone, including my parents. As a young girl I learned the behavior of pretending to be okay when I wasn't.

As an adult I had to confront the fears from my childhood. It started with first admitting that I wasn't okay with what happened. Once I expressed my anger and hurt, I had to forgive the people that hurt me. I had to release the emotions and pains I kept bottled up. I had to do the inner work and, because of this, I found the winner inside of me.

No matter what you have gone through, or what you may face, you must know that you can win. Despite what it looks like, and in spite of what it feels like, you must know that you are a winner. Life isn't easy. The more you know yourself the better you'll be at navigating the tough spots that come your way.

(F) = Focus on the Future

"Realize that our mistrust of the future makes it hard to give up the past." — Chuck Palahniuk, Survivor

To operate with a winning mentality you need to focus on the future. When you begin to put things into perspective, you keep your eyes fixed on the future. Focusing on the future keeps the circumstances of life from detouring us away from our goals. Of course, it can be hard to focus on the future when it seems as if life is throwing everything your way. Sometimes it may seem as though everything is going wrong, that there is no point in looking to the future. You can not allow your current situation, or past experiences, to determine where you go.

Don't allow past experiences to cloud your judgment. Continue to work every day at being a better version of you. Keep that winner inside of you- winning. It is very easy to lose focus when you don't know where you're going. To combat this dilemma, have a clear plan that helps keep your focus. Sometimes all you need is a little repositioning to get you back on track, to a place where you can begin focusing on your future. Be sure not to get caught up in your past. To help with this look at life as if you are in a car. On your journey you are looking through the windshield to see what is in front of you. The windshield is large and demands our focus and attention. The rearview mirror is small for a reason. This reason is so you don't get stuck looking backwards.

The dark days in my childhood became a recurring pattern. I was always facing a new dilemma with a male in life. Everything around me seemed to be going every way, but the right way. I didn't see a bright future for myself because all I felt was bleakness and depression. Because of this, I played with the idea that maybe it would be better if I was dead. For too long a moment, I was stuck with that defeated mindset. It didn't matter what people said to me, the problem was internal. Negative messages I kept telling myself were in broadcast mode, too loud for anything else to be heard. It was a very scary place to be. At that time, I didn't see a future, let alone have the ability to focus on it. I was operating in the wrong mindset.

It wasn't until I began to change my mindset, and how I looked at situations, that I was able to see and acknowledge it. I started believing in myself and my abilities. I began to repeat positive affirmations and envisioned myself as capable of overcoming. It helped me rid myself of self-defeat.

Even in the face of adversity, a winner doesn't give up, they don't throw in the towel and surrender to the woes of life. Winners stand up and keep their eyes fixed on the future because they know that is the only way to keep winning.

(E) = Eliminate your Excuses

"Ninety-nine percent of the failures come from people who have the habit of making excuses." —George Washington Carver

The next thing you will need to do, as you begin to operate with a winning mindset, is eliminate your excuses. Oh My Goodness we can come up with so many excuses as to why we can't, and won't, do something! We may use any, or all, these ideas as an excuse: I'm not pretty enough, smart enough, gifted enough, rich enough, or just plain ole I'm not enough. At the root of every excuse is one of three things, laziness, fear or lack of planning.

Growing up, how many times did you hear our parents tell you that the things you were saying were poor excuses for not wanting to do something? Well even as an adult, you still use excuses as scapegoats. Excuses are like crutches- you lean on them to take the responsibility off. You would rather make up an excuse to justify why you're not doing the very things you need, or want, to do. What other purpose does an excuse serve?

If you want to be, and stay, a winner you are going to have to take responsibility for your plan, overcome your fears and learn to self-motivate. You must get rid of every excuse that holds you back from operating with a winning mindset. How do you eliminate excuses? Figure out why you are using them in the first place. You will see how everything begins to fall into place once you overcome the default mode of excuse making.

When you use excuses, you take the easy way out. True winners don't depend on excuses they simply get the job done, or figure out alternatives, to get them to where they want to go. Plan accordingly. Set your sights on what it is that you see happening in your life. Make it happen.

Excuses won't get you out of doing the hard work. If you want to be a winner you're going to have to develop the characteristics of being a winner. If you find yourself running to excuses you have a very long way to go if you want to start producing winning results. Don't get discouraged by excuses. Make a choice to do better.

(C) = Consider the Consequences

"There are in nature neither rewards nor punishments — there are consequences."
— Robert G. Ingersoll, The Christian Religion An Enquiry

When operating in a winning mindset, or preparing to do so, consider the consequences. How many times have you done something without thinking first? How many times have you made decisions based off your emotions? Impulsive decisions are rushed decisions that leave no room for consideration of consequences. Of course, not all consequences are negative. Negative consequences occur when you don't put in the time to evaluate your choices and consider whether it will result in a favorable outcome for you.

What stops you from considering consequences? It could be that you know it's not something you should be doing. Sometimes your mind is so set on a choice that, even when faced with possible consequences, you still fail to act. This could be because you don't want to change the plans you've already made. This stubbornness forces you to make do with whatever comes along with the decision. Pride is in play when this occurs.

Another reason you may not consider the consequences is because you can't foresee a consequence that will be all that bad. This is reckless thinking. The consequences to the choices you make will not only affect you, but those around you as well. You must think about all of the consequences, and the impact they will have on your future.

If you are having difficulty checking your motives, you might want to evaluate your ability to do so when it comes to considering the consequences. I remember there was this job that I really wanted. I prayed about it and I claimed it for myself. The job required me to oversee the development of the southwest state of Florida. This meant I would be away from home and spend a lot of time traveling. I was aware of all of this but still wanted the position. I was offered the job and I was excited about it. Once in my role, after the newness wore off, I began to realize that I was missing milestones in my daughter's development. I was a single parent and I couldn't be there for her performances, events, field trips or even a mommy/daughter day. My daughter would often come to me and say, 'You can't come can you,' or 'You are the only parent that won't be there.' Hearing her say those things broke my heart. When I was making the decision to take the job, I didn't consider how the consequences would impact my daughter. I thought she would just roll with the punches. It had a negative impact on her, and ultimately me, because I was not being the mother I wanted her to have. It was very hard for me to be accountable for my actions. I had selfishly decided without considering the consequences to my relationship with my daughter. Acknowledging, and taking accountability for, the decision was not an easy task. I had created a yearning, an emptiness inside of her. Had I fully evaluated all the consequences, both positive and negative, I more than likely would have declined the offer. You can never get back time, but you can adjust where you are in the moment.

(T) = Trust God's Timing

"God is never late and rarely early. He is always exactly right on time--His time."

— Dillon Burrough, Hunger No More: A 1-Year Devotional Journey Through the Psalms

Probably the hardest thing you need to learn to do, as you develop a winning mindset, is to trust the timing of life. My faith is a cornerstone in my life and throughout my growth I have learned to trust God's timing for me. We all can be so impatient. We want everything when we want it, and how we want it. I struggled with impatience. If I wanted something done, I made sure it was done in that moment. If the person I asked was taking too long to complete my request, I would either do it myself or ask someone else to do it. This often caused relationship issues. I was not good at waiting. Patience was a hard lesson I had to learn, to incorporate into my life. This included the ability to have patience with myself. I used to want everything NOW.

I didn't understand the importance of planning, or the concept of allowing things to mature and develop. It was a long time before I realized that just because I wanted it, that didn't mean I was ready for it. I can remember about ten years ago I sat down to begin writing what would have been my first guide. I was pumped and excited about the entire thing. I had just gone through a divorce and I was ready to share my story with the world. For me, it was easier to hand write my thoughts before typing them up. People would ask, 'Why are you doing double work, writing everything first instead of just typing it out?' They said it so much I finally gave in. I stopped writing longhand and began to just type everything on my computer. A short while later, disaster struck. My entire USB drive was corrupted and I lost everything. I was crushed, and deeply hurt. All the hard work and effort I had invested in my story, was forever gone. I tried to start over, but the motivation wasn't there. Eventually I realized that it wasn't the right time.

My mom and others in my life would constantly ask, 'So when's the guide coming out?' I didn't want to throw some words on paper just to be able to say I'm an author. I wanted the words between the pages to be authentic- carefully thought out.

In 2019, something happened that sparked my desire to begin writing again. That desire manifested into the guide you have in your hand. As I reflect on my previous attempt with hindsight, two things stand out. First, I allowed others to influence me to do something the way they did it and I abandoned the thing that was working for me. I was fine handwriting my guide. It is important to listen to what you feel on the inside.

The second lesson was patience. I needed to trust God's timing. For 10 years I didn't feel inspired to write anything. I always knew there was a guide, or guides, inside of me but often wondered if I would ever feel the desire to write again.

One day I was driving home, talking on the phone with one of my mentees. As we were chatting she, in jest, asked, 'So when is the guide coming out?' She and I had never had a conversation relating to a guide. I had left that dream in my past. It was something about the way she said it, I felt my heart and spirit instantly jump. It was like her words penetrated my soul. In that moment I was inspired and my desire to write returned. The conversation we had that day stuck with me. I was ready to tackle writing again. I'm sure she has no idea how her words spoke to me that day, but they did. They awakened a sleeping dream.

You may be asking yourself, 'How will I know when it's the right time?' We all must learn to accept the timing of our life processes. Had I written the guide back in 2011, the content would not have been as developed. I wasn't healed from the pain, trauma and shame I felt when my marriage ended. I was still holding onto resentments. The baggage was wearing me down and writing from that perspective would have blurred my concept of what a winner truly is. Yes, I could have written a great personal story about how I had overcome, but I wouldn't have been able to write a guide about being a true winner. I can now write to you about surviving, overcoming and becoming a winner.

There are times when you may feel a little nudge or pull on your spirit to do, or not do, something. Some call it intuition. However, you describe it, just give it a listen. Make sure it's not the voices of people around you but a voice from within. To do this you must be tuned into your body to take notice. Don't ever forget your voice is the final voice in any decision made in your life. Trust it!

In 2011, there were a lot of lessons I had yet to learn. I'm glad that God held up on some of the things I prayed for because he understood that I was not emotionally ready to appreciate them.

When it comes to operating in a winning mindset, you must understand that patience is a big part of maturing the mindset. It is not an easy task. If you are someone who is familiar with doing what you want, when you want, you will have a very hard time achieving the ability to operate as a winner with a winning mindset until you learn to trust that things will work out in your favor. This is only the beginning of your journey to becoming a winner who wins and who operates with a winning mindset.

Before ending this chapter, I'd like you to answer the questions that follow. There are a number of exercises and questions that you will be asked to answer throughout. I want to encourage you to get a journal to write in as you continue reading this guide. I'd hate for you to run out of room for your success plan! When you finish reading this guide you'll have a book of your own; one that outlines your personal journey to success. When you master your winning journey pass your process along to someone else who can benefit from the messaging. Remember, winning is not a one-time thing or something you do sporadically. Winning is a way of life.

Ready, Set, Win.......

Below are chapter summary questions for you to answer.

List 3 key things that you took away from this chapter.

_____

_____

_____

What ways can you use the E.F.F.E.C.T. model in your life to help you win?

_____

_____

_____

_____

What personal characteristics do you have that reflect a winning mindset?

_____

_____

_____

_____

Recall a time that you were able to win in a losing situation.

_____

_____

_____

_____

Chapter 3

Winning Is A Choice

"Winners make the effort while losers make excuses."

— *Frank Sonnenberg, Soul Food: Change Your Thinking, Change Your Life*

Deciding to win, and operating with a winning mindset, is a conscious choice. You will need to put the work in and be diligent in nurturing and growing your way of thinking. You will need to be intentional about the steps you take and the decisions you make. You can choose to give up or win.

When I was getting ready to graduate from high school I was working in retail. I had previously submitted my request to take the day off for my graduation. It was a big deal to me. I guess the company I was working for did not agree. When I arrived to work for the weekly schedule, I noticed I'd been scheduled to work during graduation. I immediately brought this to the attention of my supervisor. Once I explained to her that I would not be able to work, that I had previously requested that day off, she looked at me and said, 'You will need to find someone to cover or you will have to come in and work your shift.' I absolutely could not believe the matter of fact words coming out of her mouth. It was as if she had no compassion, no understanding. She provided no reason for denying my request. I said, 'Okay. Thank you.'

I tried to find someone to fill in for me but was unsuccessful. I decided that I would not be continuing to work for a company that did not support my academic achievements. I submitted my resignation notice and told them that I would not be available to cover the shift. At that moment, I made a choice to do what was in my best interest for the betterment of my future. I could have stayed at a company that clearly didn't care too much about me, but I took control of my reality. I knew I deserved better. I couldn't allow myself to stay stuck in mediocrity and risk losing the chance to graduate with my class.

You might be asking yourself, what does this have to do with having a winning mindset? As intentional as my decision was to resign from the position, your decision to win, and operate in a winning mindset must be equally intentional. You must make a concerted effort to win. It will not always be easy. Challenges will come your way. You will need to learn to push past the hard times and overcome the obstacles in your path. You will have to trust your intuition and your gut. The more you're able to trust your instincts, your level of confidence will grow exponentially. The more confident you are will reflect in you making better decisions that can ultimately affect your destiny.

The more you begin to choose winning as a way of life, the easier it will become. It might be difficult at first, maybe even feel a bit odd, but as you consciously make decisions to win, you'll learn more about yourself. Your learning will push you to listen to yourself. That is both empowering and enlightening. As you begin to see yourself as good enough to achieve what you want for your life, you will recognize that you possess all the tools necessary to get you there.

Trusting yourself is empowering. As you make intentional winning a part of your daily life, it will begin to become a part of you. You may be saying to yourself, 'That sounds like a lot of work.' It is a lot of work; however, the effort will be well worth it.

Change comes from the inside and manifests itself outwardly. You can decide to change your life for the better. Our life is comprised solely of our choices and those choices shape our reality.

Take Chances

You owe it to yourself to do everything in your power to win. In order to be a winner, with a winning mindset, you must be willing to take chances. Taking chances can seem frightening, especially if you are used to playing it safe. How will you overcome your fear of swimming hanging out in the shallow end of the pool? You won't.

Face your fears and take a chance on you. What's the worst that can happen? You might end up living your best life or you might just stay the same. No matter how it turns out you have nothing to lose when you give it all you've got. In your past, I'm pretty sure you've taken plenty of chances that didn't have nearly as good of odds of bettering your situation. You still took the chance and did what you wanted to do. No matter how hard your goal looks, if you want to achieve it, you can.

I remember a time when I was too scared to take chances. Even now, I have to occasionally remind myself who I am when those old feelings of fear begin to creep in. When it comes to winning, and operating in a winning mindset, you have to be willing to jump- to take a leap of faith. If you have prepared, and the leap is in your best interest, it will inspire you. Take the risk. Like Nike says, just do it. At the very least you walk away inspired. That's positive momentum.

We can spend so much time helping others but when it comes to ourselves all we see are a million and one reasons why something won't work. How can you have so much faith in another person's dream, but not your own? If you reread that last line, its puzzling, right? Like wow, how can I have such a positive spirit and encourage others to live out their dreams but leave mine on the shelf?

From Rest to Action

To win we must become active and do something. Winners don't allow their lives to pass them by. They do the work and get rid of any excuses. They face their fears, and every challenge, head on. It's mind-blowing to consider where I might have been today, had I not been afraid to take risks. Not taking chances on yourself only handicaps you. Winners know how to analyze situations and make decisions based on knowledge and possible outcomes. Not every risk you take, or decision you make, will make sense. Sometimes God will speak to your spirit and you'll need to know when it's His voice and know when you should do the things that have been placed in your heart.

Just because it doesn't look like the right way, doesn't mean it isn't. Picture it like this. You have two paths in the front of you, one is clear, but you can't see what it looks like around the bend. The other is a dirt road with overgrown trees and looks a little dim. Well, what you don't see is that the road that is clear, neatly manicured, is only that way in the beginning. If you were to have traveled down that road, you would have seen that just around the bend the road became bumpy and rugged and it led to a dead end. The less appealing road, although questionable, eventually led you to a beautiful destination. Knowing all the facts, which road would you choose? I am guessing you would choose the road that led you to the beautiful destination. In other words, you can't judge the ending of a thing, based only on its beginning. This applies to any area in your life.

Face it Like a Champ

It is easy to give up, lay down and lose. It takes someone strong, someone like you, to get up and face every day like a champ. Cry yourself to sleep.

Question whether or not you have the capacity to be a winner. These too are small wins. Everyday of your life recognizing, meeting or admitting a challenge exists is the path to winning; but only if you take the extra steps to mentally transfer those lessons into positive action. Winners take the necessary steps to seek counsel to assist with the healing process when needed. That's how they heal themselves.

I mentioned earlier I was prideful, that I hated asking for help. To become a winner, I had to change that irrational way of thinking. It wasn't beneficial to me personally and it certainly wasn't helpful to any area in my life in which I wanted to thrive. Admitting I felt as though I wasn't enough was one of the reasons I found it hard to ask for help. I wanted so badly to prove to others that I was worthy that it blinded me to the need to seek assistance.

Asking for help invited the negative messages I felt about myself to surface. I didn't want to admit to others that I had the feelings I had, and I most certainly didn't want to admit these things to myself either. It took me a long time to be able to admit the extent of my internal struggles and face them like a champ. By getting real with myself, and taking the necessary steps to heal, I was conditioning and training like a champ.

You can get in the habit of questioning your ability to win. Falling into the mistaken pattern of not feeling like you are worthy of winning is a devastating error. Mistakes you've made in the past compounding with not believing you are good enough to strive for more are dangerous mindsets and excuses and according to our discussions in previous chapters you have the tools to handle those.

I am here to inspire, motivate and tell you that you are more than deserving of happiness, wholeness and healing. You can win but you have to believe that it is possible, not just some of the time but all of the time. Winning is rolling out of bed when everything inside of you is saying the covers are lonely. Winning is finding your achievement each day. Your win for the day may be getting up out of that bed and that's enough.

Because I have lupus SLE it is sometimes so painful to move that it takes me a bit to get going in the mornings. Despite this, I make it my business to give it everything I've got. If I can push past the aches and pains, that's a win. Winning isn't always big or over the top. A win can be as simple as completing a task you didn't think you had the energy for.

Wining is not giving up.

Winning is continuing to try.

Winning is pushing past your perceived limits.

Winning isn't often loud or awarded. Sometimes a win is a whisper.

Making a decision to win means you have selected winning over losing. It is my belief that if you are not doing something to progress your life then you are wasting time. Only losers waste valuable time that cannot be given back. Even if you take tiny, microscopic moves at the end of the day you are still moving.

Free Yourself from Other's Judgments

Embrace yourself for the change in your environment that this newfound way of thinking will create. People in your life may not understand you and at times you may become lonely. The transitions that will be necessary to make may mean you have to leave people, not just behaviors behind. This is okay. It will happen at some point or another. Don't worry about the naysayers, because they are going to talk anyway. Surround yourself with likeminded people who encourage your progress and are as vested in your win as you are.

Everyone who is around you is not for you. This was a very hard lesson that I had to learn. I get it, you get comfortable with the people in your life and fear losing them, or a piece of your personal history that they represent. What you postpone by keeping people in your life who are not meant to stay however, is worth evaluating. It's tough. Emotional attachments are strong. You don't want the ones in your life who aren't willing to level up, feeling as though you think you are better than them. Recognize that, to stay with them is to water yourself down to make them feel better. You must stop dimming your own light for the sake of others. I did this for years. I allowed the judgement of others to prevent me from living my life the way I wanted to live it.

Now it feels so freeing to live independently of the perception of others, but this was not an overnight occurrence for me. It took me learning who I was. It took losing some people I loved. It took me making a choice. I wouldn't have risked that if this wasn't a very important step. I am grateful that I learned it when I did because in a sense, my life is more at ease. Note, I didn't say happier. I am living my life and I don't feel like I'm walking on eggshells with the people in my life. That's progress, not happiness.

One of the things I feared when I started this guide 10 years ago was what others would think about me once they read my story. I was the pessimistic gatekeeper of my inner voice. Pessimism is an unhealthy stopgap between fear and true self. It can cause you to abandon your dreams. Knowing I always wanted to write a book, then nearly giving up on that dream, reminded me just how strong pessimism is.

So, what was my catalyst? What got this book to your shelf? Envy plain and simple. Somehow, I found out my ex-husband's mistress was writing a book. I tricked myself into thinking that I couldn't write a book because others would think I was copying, or trying to be like, her. I became pessimistic and angry. I thought, *How could she beat me at accomplishing a goal I had set for myself?* I wasn't mad because she had written a book. I was mad because of how I perceived others would view me.

Looking back, I recognize the insanity. I was willing to throw away my own dream. I was so caught up in being judged that I was ignoring the bigger picture. It was my own issues that prevented me from doing what was in my heart. The likelihood people would have judged me was slim to none. Even if people would have judged me, so what? I allowed fear to control my future. I got stuck in a world of pessimism and fear- that fear limited me. I made up unvalidated excuses. Everything I was thinking was a narrative I had created because I didn't know who I was. Had I known who I was, I would not have cared what people said about me.

Truthfully 90% of what you think others see in you isn't even on their radar. I spent so much of my life wanting and seeking approval from others. At times I disregarded my own feelings to get it. Living for others and allowing them to have that much control over my life, was draining, stressful and very unhealthy. Some may ask what would make a person live this way? The simple answer is unresolved, deep-rooted issues. Those issues can be falsely held beliefs, feeling unworthy or not enough, rejection, abandonment, lack of trust, or a myriad of other inner-core issues. I discovered I was dealing with several deeply rooted issues that began early in my childhood. One day, I realized that I was more concerned with the opinions of others than my own.

I am glad I overcame the fear of others. One of the things that led me to write this guide was finding my voice. I knew I had to get my message out after encountering so many people who were in situations where I had once found myself. They masked the pain of their life behind their careers, relationships and accolades. I remembered being that person. I wanted my stories and lessons learned to make a difference.

Not only was I afraid of what others thought, I was a people pleaser. I had to be honest with myself and learn to live in my truth. I had to stop going out of my way to do for others if it meant harming me. I had to learn to incorporate boundaries in my life and understand that not everyone in my life would like them. I could not be concerned with their opinions about the boundaries. I was doing it for my own good. Being able to live a life free of people's opinions is so much easier. I came to learn that what I often saw as their opinions of me were not well-founded beliefs. On the rare occasion when they were, I recognized that people who were unsure of themselves would attempt to manipulate me emotionally. For someone consumed with people pleasing, I often fell victim to emotional manipulation. This was another major adjustment in my life. Now I can live, and stand in, my truth. There is no more need to hide.

The act of coming to a place in your life when you are in control of your emotions will be a major shift in the way you begin to navigate this journey. We all have choices and with every choice there is a consequence bad, good or indifferent.

You have a choice to make when it comes to developing the winner in you. How are you going to govern the next set of choices placed before you? What risks are you willing to take in order to reap the benefits that come along with healing? There comes a point in the life of every winner when they stop making excuses and start making decisions that change the trajectory of their life.

Below are chapter summary questions for you to answer.

Identify three (3) reasons why you make excuses.

_____
_____
_____

Do you have any significant choices in your life that require you to make a decision? If so, what are the choices and what steps will you take to ensure you are making the best decision for your life?

_____
_____
_____

Why is it important for you to look through the front windshield of your life?

_____
_____
_____

What are two (2) main points you learned from this chapter?

_____
_____
_____

Do you think you have what it takes to be a winner and wake up choosing to win every day? If yes, what makes you say yes? If you answered no, why not? What would it take for your answer to be yes?

_____
_____
_____

Choose a personal motto to help you remember that winning is a choice.

_____
_____
_____

Chapter 4

Getting to the Root of the Issue: Doing the Work

"Everything negative – pressure, challenges – is all an opportunity for me to rise." Kobe Bryant

We all have deep-rooted issues that can taint our views of life. When I began to free myself from the judgments and perceptions of others I was ready to deal with the deep-rooted issues I'd covered up. The healed Cortina can speak freely of the things that I was once afraid to whisper. During the course of writing this book, I had to speak with my mom and dad because there were numerous things I knew I would be sharing about myself that they didn't know. After I shared with my mom some of the things I had experienced, she was in total shock and disbelief. I responded laughingly, 'Mom, it's not sad to me. It was my life and my reality. I thank God that the things I experienced no longer have me bound.' I can now walk with my head held high and know that I'm a winner regardless of what it may look like.

Before I was winning I never discussed my life much. I didn't allow myself to manage the emotions of the little girl crying inside. The little Cortina had so many questions that translated into rejection, hurt and feelings of abandonment. Those negative perceptions were inside of me as far back as I can remember. I struggled emotionally and kept it all to myself. I can remember wanting to die and just hating my life. I would often tell myself, *I hate you!* I spent a lot of my childhood confused, scared, lonely and unhappy.

From the outside looking in, my life probably appeared to be as normal as any other kid my age. I had the privilege of having both my mother and my father in my life growing up. They divorced when I was so very young that I only slightly remember them ever being together. They worked hard. I don't ever remember wanting for anything. I grew up as an only child between my mother and father, with all of my needs and wants met.

I was the apple of my father's eye and he was always there for me. He always praised me. Every time I saw or spoke to, him he would say how he was so lucky to have me as a daughter. In my father's eyes I could do no wrong. My mother was also very verbally affirming and affectionate.

In spite all this, I still struggled to find my place among my peers. For years I felt like a black sheep. I had an overarching need to appease others and to make them happy. Living life this way definitely had its pros, and its cons. I would grow to understand that the cons far outweighed the pros.

When I was in the 6th grade, I was sent to live with my aunt. At that time my family felt that was the best thing for me. My mom worked a lot and she was also in school. I can remember saying to myself, *I wish my mom was here. I just want my mom.* In no way do I blame her for not being able to be there for me. Through all the emotional stuff that I was going through, she was what, and who, I needed.

I missed my mom a lot growing up. We never had a place to call our own. Prior to moving in with my aunt, it was always just, for the most part, mom and me. My mom taught me very important lessons. I will always be grateful to her, but I was also afraid of her. I spent most of my time trying to please her and receive validation from her. I can remember only wanting my mom to be happy. There were so many emotions developing inside of me in my middle school years. There were things happening in my mother's life I didn't understand and I wasn't at liberty to talk about with anyone. No one would have understood what I was going through at that time. Due to this fact, along with the things I was watching transpire in my mother's life, I kept my pain all to myself. Everything happening in my home life is what caused me to have to go live with my aunt. This reinforced, in my underdeveloped, hormonal mind, the notion that I needed to keep my real feelings inside. Nothing was happening to me directly, however what my mother was going through had a huge impact on me. What was happening is not important to the lesson I'm sharing with you. It is not my story to tell so I won't. All you need to understand is how that time in my life impacted me as a child. After moving with my aunt, I still wanted to be with my mom so badly that I was convinced if I did not open my mouth about what I was feeling inside, I wouldn't have to leave my mom. I can remember feeling so full of overwhelming emotion the day I had to move. I just couldn't hold it in anymore. I believe, to this day, the emotional turmoil that I was feeling was magnified by my self-loathing. Those feelings led to my belief I was better off dead. All it really was, was a cry for help.

Dealing with Feelings of Inadequacy

My cousin Valencia was so pretty and everywhere we went people were always letting her know it. I wanted to be pretty like her. I wasn't jealous of her, because she was like my first best friend, but I sure did want to receive some of those compliments. She was my favorite cousin. When you saw her, you saw me. Everyone thought we were twins and would often get us mixed up all the time. We did everything together. Even though I loved her so much, I still thought I wasn't good enough, pretty enough or smart enough. Valencia was everything I wasn't. I even remember for a slight moment wanting to be her because I didn't feel good in my own skin.

When I was in the 5th grade, I remember thinking to myself, *'Why doesn't anyone like me?'* What I was really asking was, *'Why don't boys want to date me?'* Even though I didn't want a boyfriend I did want one of them to have a crush on me, or at least think I was cute! Maybe it was all in my mind, but it seemed as if everyone always seemed to come to me in order to get to my cousin. This was elementary school so there were no 'real' boyfriend/girlfriend relationships going on, just innocent crushes. In my mind, I was known as the funny goofy one. Looking back, I can see how my perception may have been a bit skewed. I don't know why I was feeling the way I was because everyone thought Valencia and I looked alike. As I got older and entered middle school, I put on the funny, goofy girl as my identity mask. During that time, that was my reality, the way I viewed myself. I never quite felt good enough.

As far back as I can recall, I felt as though I was always being compared to others. This was due to both the things I would hear from others and the internal messages I would tell myself. This was the birth of my feelings of inadequacy. Whether it was myself doing the comparing or someone else, me just being me, made me feel like I was incomplete. I felt as though I was always being compared to Valencia, as if me being me was not enough. The truth is I did not always love, or even like, myself for who I was. I thought I was ugly. I thought my teeth were too big. I thought my feet were too big. I was sickly. I didn't think I was really all that smart. I was very goofy and quirky and different. I settled on the notion that maybe I was just meant to be the funny one of the group.

I wanted everyone to like me so much that it became an obsession. I would go out of my way to be nice to people. I thought if they liked me, maybe they would accept me and not truly see how broken or unhappy I felt inside. I was always very friendly and outgoing. I liked everyone for the most part. I didn't like confrontation and I've always wanted everyone to get along. I used my smile and humor as a mask to hide the crying little girl inside.

When I was in high school I began cutting myself. It made me feel better. It was the thing in my life that I had control over. One time I got scared because I went a little too deep. I still have the scar on my calf as a reminder of the pain I was feeling back then.

Everything I experienced in my life, contributed to the creation of the messed-up woman, who felt as though she and she alone, was not enough. I was overwhelmed with anxiety. I had to stop and realize that I had lived a life but hadn't been honest about who I was. Heck, I didn't even know who I was. I was someone who lived my life to please others. I spent most of my time proving to people who weren't even important to me, that I was enough. I came to realize that I needed to make the adjustment. I needed to know at my core that I, and I alone, was enough.

Am I Good Enough?

I went fishing with my stepdad and stepbrother on a school holiday. Before mom left for work she told me I better know all of my spelling words when she got home. I remember studying them on the way to the fishing spot. It seemed like it took us forever to get there. I tried to study on the way back too, but it had gotten too dark. I tried to study while fishing, but my mind was too distracted. I remember being nervous because I knew I didn't know how to spell some of the words. I kept spelling them wrong when I would try on my own. I wasn't prepared for the test my mom would be giving when she came home from work that night after her 12-hour shift.

Mom came home and called me into her room. I knew she would want me to spell the words for her. The hall seemed to get so long! Even though the house size was exactly the same as it had always been, it was the longest walk of my short life. I was standing against the wall as she sat on her waterbed with the list of words in-hand, ready to call them out. She gave me the test spelling bee style. I can't spell like that. I never could and she knew it. She should have allowed me to write them down, but it wouldn't have mattered, I still wasn't prepared. After I failed miserably, she spanked me because I didn't know how to spell the words. Now, before your mandated reporting antenna starts to go up, I was not physically abused by my mother. I repeat, I was not an abused child.

For the life of me I couldn't understand why she spanked me for not knowing my words that evening. It wasn't even the school's test. It was her own. She could easily have identified the words I needed to practice so I could pass the test at school. During that encounter my mom said, 'You want to be like your cousin so much why don't you try to get the grades she gets?' My heart sank. Worse than the pain from the spanking was the pain from hearing those words.

The Comparison

The comparison to my cousin was then etched in my mind. The sense of *I'm not enough* was deepened. Valencia was the perfect student. She made straight A's. She had perfect attendance and never missed a day of school ever... not one. She never got into trouble and, she even had beautiful hands and nails. I was always the sick one. I had asthma so I couldn't run fast, and I would snort when I laughed. So when my mom said those words, my feelings were hurt. From that moment I tried to please my mother and make her proud. I never wanted her to be mad at me. I wanted her to see me through the same eyes she saw my cousin. I wanted to please her, and anyone else whose approval I sought. I felt inadequate, as if what I had to give was not enough. That was the springboard of what would be an area of contention in my later years.

For the longest time, I defined who I was by my performance and presentation. I became super critical of myself. It became highly unhealthy. I would encourage any parent to evaluate the unintended messages your lessons may give to your children. As an adult, I know my mom meant no harm. That doesn't change how I felt, and the lasting impact it had on my life.

Those negative thoughts followed me to college. I often speak to my patients about how detrimental not dealing with the root of the problem can be. One would think that someone can eventually just get over it. Well that's now how our minds work. We don't just get over stuff or heal without doing some type of work. If you feel that you have healed from trauma or negative past experiences, you are only kidding yourself. You may have suppressed the feelings but, trust me, anything that comes along that reminds you of the situation can activate the unresolved emotions at any time.

When I was a junior in university, I remember getting an A- on my report card and totally losing it. I was crying as if the world was ending. I felt like I was failing myself because I didn't get an A+. My logic was my GPA would be messed up and that somehow would determine how good of a person I was. This was how I was viewing myself. To me it meant that I was less than, not good enough. This was because I did not know who I was outside of how I performed.

Performance Based Recognition

Almost all of my self-validation came from performance-based recognition. Performance-based recognition is when someone recognizes the hard work, or effort, you put into an assignment or task. It was my way of being validated and, in some way, seeking approval from anyone I felt was in a superior position. This was a very common theme in my life. Basing my identity on how I performed pushed me in certain areas, but it also handicapped my ability to develop a true sense of self-esteem. I was an overachiever. That got me far in my professional life. Everything about me became performance based. As I got older nothing in my life mattered except my career and doing well. The downside of that was I neglected other areas necessary to have a balanced, full life. My career was a means of escaping things happening in a personal life that I had built with far less effort.

I had this big personality and strong presence. I came across as an overly confident woman. In reality what I wanted was acceptance. I was doing those things and accomplishing all of those goals to set myself apart, but I wasn't happy. I was overcompensating for what I was lacking on the inside. Even when I was accepted by others, I was still rejected by myself. No matter how much recognition I gained, I was still questioning if I was really living up to the standards of others. I always wanted to be the best at, or at the top of whatever it was that I was doing. Even at the top I realized the same questions lingered and I still didn't know what I was truly searching for.

Thankfully I overcame my performance based recognition cycle. Is this something you struggle with as well? It's common among high achieving individuals. A few ways to stop basing your worth on performance-based recognition would be to ask yourself, why is other's approval or recognition so important to you? The next thing you will need to ask yourself is, if you don't get the recognition, does that somehow mean the work or effort you put into the project was in vain? Lastly, you will need to work in separating yourself as a person from how you perform. You are not on the stage every minute of your life. Your worth, and self-acceptance can't come solely from the validation of others. This is why it is imperative that you get to know yourself.

One of the most important things I want you to grasp from this chapter is the fundamental principle of getting to know who you are. This does not include who people say you are, or who you think they think you are, but who you know yourself to be. Until you can do that, you will never be able to make the necessary adjustments to become a true winner.

It's tough to sit with all your pain, and look at your life, while trying to understand your core being. This is one of the reasons why people have therapists. Do what you need to do to heal you so that the real winner inside can finally stand up. Don't allow past situations to make you become jaded. Shed the masks that you wear every day and learn to love yourself.

As you continue in your development as a winner, reflect on any deeply held mistrust issues that may be affecting you today. When we fail to resolve the core of our trust issues deeper issues may emerge in our relationships causing depression, fear of rejection, or feelings of unworthiness or that we are unlovable. You may also connect the impact of past traumatic experiences, and how the negative effects of the events are still showing up in your life today.

Below are chapter summary questions for you to answer.

List potential barriers that may prevent you from being able to identify the root cause of your issues.

_____
_____
_____
_____

List 3 personal things about yourself that you have never shared with anyone else and think about the reasons behind keeping these things to yourself.

_____
_____
_____
_____

Have you ever experienced anything traumatic from your childhood or early adulthood that changed your perception of the world, or of who you were?

_____
_____
_____
_____

Has there ever been a time when you felt inadequate or as if you're alone? Have you ever felt you were not enough?

_____
_____
_____
_____

If there is anything that you need to do to heal? What is it that needs to be done?

_____
_____

_____
_____

At your core, who are you?

_____
_____
_____
_____

Chapter 5

Winners are Honest: Live Out Your Truths

"You can never be true to others, if you keep on lying to yourself."
— *Gift Gugu Mona*

What does it really mean to live in your truth? To me, it means getting real about my intentions, motives, desires, needs and feelings about the things occurring in my life. It means letting myself be vulnerable and teachable. It means tending to my needs before I attend to anyone else's. It means the emotional side of me is nurtured and cared for. It means healing my past and making the necessary adjustments, when needed, for the sustainability of my future. This was hard for me to do, until it was the only thing left for me to do. I want you to define what living out your truth means to you. As you start to deal with the root of a problem you should now be comfortable expressing not only what happened, but how it affected you. One of the limitations of living out the truth is the vulnerability it will require to go through the healing process.

This is an area where you will need help. Dealing with my truth meant accepting that I was allowed to express anger, hurt and grief. Living out my truth meant I could ignore the lie that I always had to be the strong person for everyone else. No one ever told me I was required to be strong but I felt like I had to live up to society's stereotype of what it meant to be a strong woman all the same. I didn't know how to ask for help. I assumed if I was strong I wouldn't need help. Not asking for help, while thinking you are strong, does not make you a winner. Thinking I had to always be strong and having that belief reinforced caused me to behave in ways I wish I hadn't.

Big Girls Don't Cry

Tragedy struck our family and the one person I loved the most, Valencia, was dying. I was devastated. We had so many good memories. I received a call from my mother telling me that Valencia had, had a seizure and was being rushed to the hospital. I was 4-hours away by car. I told my mom, 'I'm on my way.' Everything was going through my mind as I was driving. *I just spoke to her this morning. This can't be happening. She doesn't even suffer from seizures. I can't get there fast enough.* Never, never, never, not even in my wildest dreams, would I have guessed I would never hear my cousin's voice again.

When I arrived at the hospital, I definitely was not prepared for what I saw. I saw a chaplain and instantly became upset. I asked what he was doing there. They told me it was just customary. This made me a bit suspicious. I got myself together to go see her and, when I walked in the room, I immediately collapsed. They had to pick me up off the floor. I saw her on a ventilator and blood was everywhere from their attempt at thinning out the blood clot. As they carried me back into the lobby I was crying. My grandma said to me, 'Alright now. It doesn't take all of that. We don't need that noise.' I couldn't believe what I was hearing. I was hurting, I felt like part of me was dying too. I needed to express my heartache. I stopped crying. When I did cry, it was a silent cry. I was so heartbroken and sad.

Nothing in my life, past or present, was harder on me than seeing her like that. A part of me felt guilty because I was the sick one, I was the one, if anybody, who should have been in her place. I remember not wanting to question God but asking, thinking to myself, *Why her?*

I was told that she had a pulmonary embolism. I can remember being encouraged to go say my goodbyes. The first time I attempted to walk back down the hallway, I was only able to make it to halfway. I couldn't do it. It was too painful. The next time I tried, I pushed myself to be strong. My cousin Tiffany and I stood by her bed and talked to her. She was not able to respond. The machine breathed for her. By this time she had already coded 4 times. I rubbed her hand apologizing to her for all of the blind dates I had set her up on, and thanked her for always being my right hand. I was just rambling because I really had no words. I told her that I would be sure to watch over her daughter Aaliyah and to always be there for her. In the midst of this the nurses asked if we could leave for a bit so they could do a shift change. I told Valencia that I would be right back. Unfortunately, for me, that never happened. They called for us to go back to her floor. I can remember my mother coming to me and saying, 'She's gone.' This was the day my heart stopped. I was in shock and I was numb. I cried the entire night. She was just one month shy of her 30th birthday. She was so young, full of life, but she was gone.

The words of my grandmother, somehow sent a message to me that I needed to be proper, stop my grieving and act right. I am sure she probably said those words to comfort me, but I filtered her words through my own experiences and expectations. No matter her intentions, for me her words had a different meaning, and that meaning had a lasting effect. Even after my cousin's passing, at her funeral and wake, I held myself together, not being as emotional as I would have liked to have been. This was largely due to the comment my grandmother had made. I was devastated by the passing of my cousin. She was my everything. Not grieving her the way I wanted extended my grieving process. I would cry when I was alone but I would not outwardly sob like my heart wanted. I was being a good girl, doing what my grandma requested of me. I needed to do what was right for me. In some strange way I felt as though if I did show outward emotions, I would somehow shame or embarrass the family. My grandmother's words had stifled my grieving process and I unknowingly built up resentment.

Part of being honest with yourself is being honest with others. When we live for others and do something contrary to what we really want to do, we begin to hold resentment in our hearts. Holding onto resentment is an indication that, that area in your life is not yet healed. You must heal those areas, and begin to speak your truths, so that you can adjust and become open to discovering other things that have not been resolved. Take time to get to know yourself so that you can identify the areas that need work. If I would have known myself like I do now I would have handled the situation with my grandmother totally differently. I would have been respectful, but I would have expressed my grief the way that was right for me.

Growth and Adjustments

The realization of self is a necessary growth and adjustment process for any winner. Over time you'll begin to notice your transformation as you start to question why you behave in certain ways. Winners make the necessary adjustments to their lives on their road to becoming. Growing is a part of the necessary process. I did not see it back then, but everything that I have experienced has, in some way, helped me to grow. Through my growth, adjusting my perception was a part of the process. Adjusting is not a one-time thing. You will need to adjust yourself, your perceptions, your expectations, your focus and your outlook, as things continue to happen in life. My feeling like I could not outwardly express my sorrow reinforced my belief that I had to be strong at all times. I came to realize that I began to hate the very notion of what it meant to be a strong woman. I didn't want the responsibility of being forced to be strong. Even having and shedding this mindset was a part of the growth process. It wasn't until I was able to grow that I realized the way I took my grandmother's words was not the way she intended them.

There were plenty of other times in my life where I played a part or pretended to be more than what I was. I would wear growth as a garment taking it off and putting it on when needed. This too was part of the problem. Deep down inside I was still unhealed.

Adjustments are necessary. It will be essential to make adjustments because they help you continue to grow. Even now I still find myself adjusting as needed. Don't be alarmed about the people that are going to get mad at you as you begin to make your adjustments. Let them. You must begin to live for you. Learn to get honest about who, and what, hurt you so that you can process, adjust and move forward in your life. When this happens healing can take place and that is what is needed in order to be free and live in your truth.

As we begin to speak, and live with, our truths we are emotionally removing the shackles placed upon us by others, real or imagined. As we face resentment, we realize our inability to state our truth makes it harder for us to be our authentic selves. We must be willing to face who we are, and our role in getting ourselves there, in order to fix the areas that need to be fixed. I concluded at the start of my winning process that I'm okay losing everything in my life except myself. No more will I allow what people think of me, or who they thought I was, to plague my mind. Change can be hard for anyone. Risking your happiness, just because something appears to be hard, is just not worth it. Make the adjustments that need to be made. You'll thank yourself later. I had to learn to be my own best friend first. I had to learn to figure out what made me happy. I had to spend time alone in order to get to know myself better.

What is Your Truth?

For many, many years I didn't know my truth. I would pretend to know, but honestly, I had no idea. I had to hold the mirror up and continue to make adjustments until I was content with being the way I was. Many people avoid looking in mirrors because they don't like looking at who they are. They avoid mirrors because they reveal their failures, past mistakes and disappointments. They continue to pretend, to be who they are not, until that imposter part of them overtakes them and becomes who they then see reflected back. Take time to figure out what you need to change and what steps will be needed to ensure that change takes place in your life.

I was an incredibly open, yet closed, person. I know you are wondering, what the heck does that mean? That simply means like most people, I told people what I didn't care about them knowing but I kept 75% of my personal information to myself. One of the reasons for this was my fear of people's judgment. There were so many things that happened in my life that, until recently, I had never told a soul. If you knew me prior, you would have thought, 'Wow her life is great and she's so positive.' The truth is, I was, and I still am a very positive person. The truth is also that I was hiding my pain and I kept a lot of my internal struggles to myself.

When I would tell people all about my health struggles, I would list them very matter-of-fact. I later realized I was very detached from the events, and circumstances, of my life. I had survived the things life had thrown at me, but I hadn't processed them, or the emotions behind them. I hadn't dealt with my true feelings. Hell, I didn't even know what my feelings were. They were on the back burner.

I am a very emotionally sensitive person but things that would have devastated some, didn't even cause me to flinch. That was not normal. I thought it was a testament of how strong I was, but it highlighted how weak, and out of touch with my own reality, I was. I thought if I emulated strength that somehow people wouldn't judge me, that they wouldn't see me as less than. I thought it would affect my credibility as this strong, capable person if people saw my weak side. I wondered if I would not be viewed a winner or survivor, because of my connection with my human emotions. Whether it was one or all of these things, it wasn't healthy.

I was somehow basing my ability to be real against my fear of judgement from others. I felt like I had to be perfect, I had to hit the mark every time. All of this stemmed from seeds that were planted in my mind during childhood. What I needed as a child was therapy. How could I have gotten the help I needed if I continued to keep everything to myself? Closed lips don't get fed. I had perfected the art of pretend. Everyone assumed that I had a healthy, happy childhood. I used to be very secretive and selective about the things I shared.

At this point in my life however, I don't care about the opinions of others. I am no longer willing to give other people's judgements control over my happiness. With this comes the ability to set boundaries in your life. You have to be able to let people know that you are not looking for their approval. Every area of your life is not open to debate, input or speculation. This goes for family, friends, children, everyone. I am not saying disregard sound advice and be reckless with your life. I am saying why let someone's opinion on what you have going on in your life prevent you from moving forward. They may be projecting their own fears and insecurities onto you. You can't negate your own feelings indefinitely. I spent many years doing it. Looking back, I don't regret it because moving on from that taught me so much about myself. I also became okay with my side of a story never being told. Who did I have to prove anything to? Why did it matter so much how people saw me? If my heart and mind are clear, that's all that matters.

Most of what you see on television and in social media is disingenuous. Don't become a casualty of the society of fakeness, we are living in. Don't airbrush yourself and lose the real you in the process. You are beautiful and deserving of everything good that is coming your way, you are not required to believe it, not yet anyway. If you want better for your life, that starts with a belief that you deserve it. In order to get there you must work through the painful process of taking off the mask.

Become a maskless winner in a world full of impostors. Strip off the designer clothes, make up, suits, Italian-made handbags, clothing labels or any other item you feel the need to accessorize yourself with and see what you look like. Who is lying underneath? Begin to reveal the true you that's covered by your car, cash, status and accolades. If all those things were stripped from you, how would you define yourself? To be able to sit comfortably with yourself, you must know who you are outside of those external things. Without those things would you feel inadequate or inept? Don't allow material things to define who you are as an individual.

Understanding that your perceived failures are not a reflection of who you are is a must. You are not going to win at everything in life. You are still a winner. How do you begin to take challenging situations head on? You start by recognizing that no one can be good at all things. Sometimes you are better off knowing your weaknesses than your strengths. When you do, act accordingly. Your knowledge of self is your strength. Think about it, you can't claim you know yourself then turn around and beat yourself up because you weren't able to perform a task the way you had hoped. What you can do is try again! Ask for help if you need it or give it your full attention if you were slacking off the first go around. Once you get rid of old patterns of thinking begin to live and walk with your true self, this won't be difficult to do.

One of the biggest failures you will have to tackle is facing the fact that you have failed yourself. You stopped loving yourself. You stopped caring for yourself. You stopped believing in yourself. You stopped encouraging yourself. You stopped your own emotional growth.

I am so blessed that I was able to learn this concept. All the things I faced in my life that caused me to build walls, had to be processed and worked through in order for the walls to be knocked down. Even though I'm not where I used to be in this department, I'm still not a perfect person. Navigating through all of this was no easy feat. As I began to work on my stuff, and began the process of taking off the mask, I had to face some hard truths that I didn't want to deal with. It was hard but necessary for my emotional growth, and the development of my better self. I had to explore the reasons for the walls and masks I hid behind.

Who wants to admit that they are weak or even not as strong as people think?

Who wants to admit that there were times when sleeping was better than being awake?

At least when I was asleep it allowed me time to ignore my inner pain, hurtful truths and the scars of misfortune.

Who wants to admit to fears and discontentment?

I didn't want to face it, but I did. I'm no longer ashamed to talk about who I am and present the truest version of me.

Below are chapter summary questions for you to answer.

What does living in your truth, mean to you?

___

Have you been honest about yourself regarding the things in your life? If not, what are the things you have not been honest with yourself about?

___

Do you have the courage to face your past and speak your truth to those in your life who have hurt you?

___

What adjustments in your life are needed in order for you to win?

___

What are your thoughts on change and adjusting? How will you begin to make the necessary adjustments in your life to help find the winner in you?

___

How do you view the judgments of others and how do they affect your life?

_____
_____
_____
_____
_____

Chapter 6

Removing the Masks

"I think that's the most important thing you can do to be a real person – is to be honest with yourself.

~ Mike Dirnt, Musician Green Day

At this point in the guide, I want you to reflect on your personal life for a moment. I have shared many of my personal experiences to help you feel more comfortable with the process. From here on out I want you to start identifying the areas that need your attention. As you read this chapter, challenge yourself to discover things within that need adjusting. This will not be easy. It's not always easy to be honest with ourselves because, often times, we don't like or love what we see when we begin to take off the masks we're wearing, the ones that hide our dorky, silly, uncoordinated, not all-together selves from the world.

I was the queen of wearing masks. The masks I wore were as big as my personality. I often sat with myself and asked, *'How could someone so smart and bubbly be so bound and lost?'* I wanted to be everything to everyone. I wanted to make everyone proud and everyone happy because, in my own warped mind, that helped me fill the void of feeling like I wasn't enough. Most of my life I can remember having to prove myself. For what reason, I'm still not sure. When I started working in corporate America, it only worsened. I often felt misunderstood in an industry dominated by other ethnicities. I felt like they were reading me wrong and that made me feel like I had to prove why I too deserved a seat at the table. If I made a mistake, I would obsess over it. I would replay it over and over in my mind. I would lose sleep over it. I somehow began to think that making a mistake was a direct reflection of who I was. Although that may have been who I was at the time, as I continued to mature, I realized that I did not have to be bound by the mistakes of my past.

You cannot get caught up in thinking the choices you make permanently define who you are as an individual. I tell my patients this all the time. It took me a long time to get this. I was only able to get this after I healed the hurt of being bound by and living for others. I had to learn to love myself and change the things about me that needed to be changed. Life is so much more freeing now that I've had the opportunity to get real with myself.

Expecting the Unexpected

You never really know when your life is going to take another direction. Be ready. It will come. When it does you need to have your coping skills fine tuned. Had you asked me prior to the development of this guide what would I do if I were to be fired, I would have responded by saying something like, 'OMG I'd die.' Well, I'm here to tell you it happened. I'm still here and I'm not only stronger for it, I'm better for it too.

You are stronger than you know. When you learn to trust the process you can rest knowing things will always work out. If what you are facing is too hard, know that it is okay to reach out and ask for help.

No matter how hard life may seem it is your responsibility to yourself to believe that you have the power to deal with it. You may get knocked down, you may even lay on the ground for a while but in the end, oh you better believe you will get back up. I'm not going to act as though life can't be hard and painful, I am encouraging you to commit yourself to be better, to do better every day. If you think something you are facing will never get better, well you've guessed it, it won't.

Have faith that what you are going through is a lesson you need to help you navigate to your next level of greatness. How you perceive challenges determines what you do about them. I thought I was losing my job when

I was really gaining so much more. That thing I was holding on to for dear life, the thing that was in the forefront, and at the expense of everything in, my life was holding me back. It acted as a barrier to my elevation. God cannot bless us with more if we are unwilling to free our hands so he can put his blessings in them.

When you don't let go because of fear, that fear becomes paralyzing. It stunts your emotional and mental growth. It keeps you in a comfort zone, but all the best things happen when you test your own margins. When you fear you don't take risks. You stay in the shallow end of the pool where you can see your feet. I want you to know that you won't really begin to develop until you begin to take risks. A leap of faith is the antidote to any fear you face.

You mentally, emotionally and spiritually grow when things in your life are unknown. You grow during these times because you begin to find solutions. Freed from the constraints of a box, crisis pulls creativity out of us. We are forced to improvise. Had every road in life been clear, you would not have had some of the blessings you have been able to experience happen in your life. This is a lesson I continue to work through every day. I remember being so scared to fail that I was only holding up my own future. What are you risking? Is it a sacrifice you're willing to make or is it time to elevate higher?

Acceptance

I had to accept that the person I was masking was an actual part of me. I had to embrace her with open arms so that she felt supported and safe enough to come out of hiding. I had to practice what I preached to my patients. I had to take time out for me to get to know all the aspects of my personality, even the not so pleasant parts, because they too were a part of me. You will need to learn to love yourself a little more every day. Be kind to yourself and never underestimate the power of being patient.

There may be times when you try to run from yourself. Avoiding who you are is a protective measure. Think about someone who leaves home and never comes back. They may go somewhere else and reinvent themselves. It is possible they have not healed the thing that caused them to run in the first place. What about the person who tries to hide where they came from and protect their past from coming out at all? This is a person who has not dealt with why they felt the need to hide a part of their whole.

I am not implying that it is unhealthy to want to get away from your surroundings. What I am saying is make sure you are not doing so in an effort to deny, or avoid parts of your whole. If you do that, you will never be able to begin living in your truth. While this is not the case for everyone, it certainly is for a lot of people. If you see things differently, this is a tale tell sign that the situation(s) you've faced have changed you.

Facing who you truly are can be the scary side of becoming a winner. To win, you must operate as one in every area of your life. You don't want to be a partial winner. It's a season, not a game. One win isn't a complete transformation.

Do what you need to in order to heal yourself and win. Part of this is owning up to, and taking responsibility for, who you are. I had to realize that there were things I had allowed in my life that caused some of my downfalls. I focused a lot on my career and this was at the forefront of my life. I would literally go 1000% when it came to how I performed at work. I had to realize that, although I was efficient and great at what I did, the motivation behind it was based in the unresolved core issue of feeling like I wasn't enough. It was my way of proving my worth.

My mom would often ask, 'why are you so dedicated to your job? If something were to happen to you, before you were buried, they'd have someone to fill your position.' This bothered me because I knew she was right. Why was I sacrificing my work life balance for the sake of someone else's success? I've always been extremely motivated and dedicated, that wouldn't change. She was trying to teach me that there always needs to be balance. I can remember not being able to do things or go places because I felt that it meant I was better than others when I could use the excuse 'I have to go to work.' Most times, there was no one telling me I had to go. I chose to go because of my loyalty to the company and to my patients. Where was that same loyalty to myself and my family? Somehow my mind equated that my being there, going above and beyond, would prove to my employer just how much of a hard worker I was. I couldn't rest on my productivity speaking for itself.

I based a lot of how I saw myself on how well I performed. As I've mentioned throughout this guide these beliefs were formed in my childhood and reinforced as I aged. I needed to look at how these beliefs were dictating the decisions I made in my life and what that meant for me moving forward. My life was my career. Everything in my life revolved around the positions I held. I had worked hard to get to where I was, and was proud of my professional status. It defined my self-worth. There was always a fear, deep down inside of me that if I lost the thing that I felt defined me, I would lose it all. I would often ask myself, *'What would you do if you lost your job?'* I really thought that losing my position would be one of the most devastating things in my life. Little did I know, I was about to get the shock of a lifetime and I never saw it coming.

I was finally feeling, for once in my life, that my career and love life were in sync. I was traveling. I was happy. I was comfortably content. Little did I know, that was all about to change. I was forced to face who I was, and my idea of who I was, would be tested. My life was about to be turned upside down.

The thing I'd always feared was happening. It was something I hadn't expected. It was something I had no control over. It was as if everything I had worked hard for was ripped away from me in an instant. Even now, I can still hear the words, 'We regret to inform you that we have decided to rescind the offer previously extended to you.' Just like that I was unemployed. The thing I'd worked so hard for, my sense of security was pulled out from under me. I was stuck. One of the lessons I learned through this experience was not to put my all into something that wasn't guaranteed. I was trying to make sense of what was happening. Quickly, my mind was filled with so many questions. I found myself trying to make sense of the confusion happening in my mind. I could not swallow my reality in the moment. I was numb. I was hurt. I was in complete shock. After all I had done for that company, I put all of me into their success.

I'm not saying don't put your heart into what you do. I'm saying set boundaries for your life. Don't overlap your work and personal life. You need to understand that your security cannot be attached to something that can be so easily taken away. You should find ways to vest your sense of power in what is within your control. Looking back, I can see that the thing I feared the most is the very thing that needed to happen. It caused me to grow in ways I wouldn't have tried to, had it not.

I am so thankful to have lived through all of that and still be here to share how far I've come, to teach you how I became honest with myself. When you continue to wear masks, who you are wearing them for and what purpose they serve are vital questions to address. They serve a single purpose, to cover the insecurities within us and dim our true ability to shine. If you are doing this in the name of another then you have a toxic relationship with either that person or yourself. Either way, things need to change.

Discovery

It wasn't until I lost my job that I realized a lot of my self-identity was tied into my career and the positions I'd held. Without those titles I was, in a way, stuck. I remember being asked, 'So what do you do?' I was stumped. I didn't know how to answer the question. Even though I had been offered a job, it wasn't one with a title. Despite it not being my fault that I was unemployed, I was embarrassed not to have a job. Until the day my position was terminated, I had been employed since the age of 14. I was walking into a season in my life that would test everything I had taught my patients. Now it was my turn to test my own theories. How would I handle the unknown? Would I know how to navigate this road less traveled? It was the only path currently in front of me so I had no choice.

I believe that had I not begun to work on myself, on healing my past pains, that my ability to handle what I previously thought would have killed me would have been far more difficult to manage. It also highlighted my need for security, something that had not been on my list of things to address before then. While many of the things we battle can be directly traced back to our childhood, we are children no more. I had to let go of my past pain to diminish the effect those experiences had on my future. It is so important that you begin by healing those areas.

You cannot make excuses for why you don't begin the healing process. You can't keep playing the part, pretending to be something you aren't. Pretending to have it all together is a heavy burden to bear. Core issues are the inaccurate beliefs we have about ourselves. They include insecurities; feeling worthless, unworthy, not enough, inadequate, unlovable; an inability to trust, and self esteem. On your journey, I want you to identify what core issues you may need to resolve. Once they have been identified, you will be better prepared for making a switch.

After reading this guide, all your excuses for not working on yourself should be eliminated. Never give up on your quest to better yourself. You owe it to yourself to keep going, to become the winner you were created to be. No one else can do it for you. You can't keep up the act of playing the part. That's no longer going to serve you if your desire is to go higher and further. You will have to elevate. Don't be afraid of what can happen. Begin adjusting your life by processing and healing your past. Some of the things you are holding on to may be the very things hindering your growth. Don't be afraid to let go. Stop hiding behind who you used to be and start walking in who you were created to be. Often time, we become afraid to be real with ourselves about the things we have failed to accomplish. We ignore our mistakes, and past failures become future problems because we are not facing parts of ourselves that need to change. It is important to get to know yourself. Once you know who you are, you will be able to communicate who that is to others in a way that is a reflection of your true self.

Effective Communication

There were times when I did not effectively communicate my needs or boundaries. This caused me to do things that I did not feel like doing. For example, I really didn't like talking on the phone or even answering my phone. This was mostly due to the fact that I used my voice all day at work and when I was done for the day, I really just wanted to relax and not have to use my voice more than necessary. Because I did not communicate that to the people in my life it caused some issues. When you know who you are, and are okay with being who you are, it is not hard to communicate that to others. Sometimes we do things we don't want to then, midway through, we stop because that isn't who we are. That shift in dynamic can cause people to think we've switched up on them. Know who you are and be consistent.

Because I was a people pleaser, I would often time do things I really didn't want to do just so people wouldn't get mad at me. Where I am in my life now, I make sure that I'm not forcing myself to do anything. Being too nice leads to me feeling walked over. This was one of the issues that I had to resolve. I wanted to be everything to everyone. That wasn't healthy for me, or anyone else for that matter. I had to learn to be okay with knowing that everything was not in my control, no matter how hard I wanted it to be.

Releasing

Control was also a major issue for me. I wanted to be in control of everything. When people feel out of control in their lives they may focus on a specific area within their control, to help alleviate the uncomfortable feelings. Some of the things I did, and decisions I made were directly influenced by the amount of control I felt I had. I shut down and kept things in. I should have been sharing myself, instead I protected myself by controlling what I did with the information. When I worked more than I should have, I was trying to control my narrative and people's perception of what kind of employee I was. When I kept my guard up and kept people at arm's length, it was me trying to keep from getting hurt. While trying to control everything in my life, and preventing pain from entering, I had to ask myself a very hard question, *What are you searching for and what will you do when you find it?* I was looking for a guarantee that no one else would hurt me the way I had been hurt in my past. I was looking for peace. I wanted to feel happy about who I was. I was looking for the young unharmed girl. She needed to remind me it would all be okay. I was looking for one thing to fill all the voids I felt inside. I was looking for me, the person I had lost so many years ago.

I spent so much of my life running away from who I was that I ended up becoming someone I didn't know. I placed my pain on a shelf and walked away from it. I left it there, rotting my insides and wishing it would disappear. I was able to encourage and motivate my patients, my staff, but I wasn't taking my own advice. As I would teach lessons, I realized that I was also talking to myself. The toughest lesson to learn was that there was no way for me to have everyone, and every situation, under control. I had to learn to breathe, relax and release. There are no guarantees in life. The idea that we are on offense, controlling the outcome of our lives is unrealistic. We don't control what happens in our lives. The best way to have control is to create a solid defensive plan that has latitude to respond to numerous situations.

For many years I searched to find where I belonged, where I fit. It wasn't until I got real about who I was that I found it. I don't regret one bit taking time away from simply existing to get to know the real me. I began to understand my emotional wellbeing could not be based on the feelings of others, or how I thought they saw me.

Healing and Breaking Through

I no longer try to fit in or pretend that I am someone I'm not. I learned who I was and I am able to walk proudly and boldly in that skin. You must be willing to do the same. The same amount of energy you put into hiding who you are, reverse it. Harness it for good. Don't allow fear to prevent you from discovering yourself. Until I was able to discover my true self, I was not able to fulfill my destiny. You must learn to reflect on your life and to identify the things still holding you back and then release yourself from its grip.

I was the master at keeping secrets, but I later learned that keeping secrets came at a price. How much have you paid by not being true to yourself? I missed out on a lot of things because my fake self was the one experiencing the happy times. My real self was someplace in the background hiding. It's time for your real self to come out from behind the mask. It is time for you to discover your inner virtues and be comfortable in your own skin. Mastering this takes time, so be patient with yourself. Don't rush the process and get stuck thinking it will never happen for you. This was a lesson I had to learn. When I would become overwhelmed, I would retreat and shut down. This happened as a result of me not being able to be honest with myself or with others. If I was unable to be honest with myself, how on earth was I ever going to be honest with other people?

Get rid of your fear of judgment by others if that is your issue. Separate how you see yourself from the way you believe others see you. Clean, adjust or replace the lenses you have been filtering yourself through. Once you can accomplish this task, you will be better able to stay true to you. Here are a few suggestions to help you prepare for your breakthrough:

1. Journal your emotions, thoughts, feelings and experiences.
2. Take regular self-inventory so that you stay on top of the things that need tweaking.
3. Be honest with yourself. You have to if you are going to be a winner who operates with a winning mindset.

Consider everything outlined in this chapter and apply it to your life as needed. You don't truly know who you are until you spend time learning, exploring, discovering and developing yourself. Stop hiding. Come out from behind your masks. Shed the layers of shame, fear and guilt that cloud the real you. Allow your light to shine because you've been dimming it for far too long. Be an authentic version of you. Remain patient and trust the process. It won't be easy, but it will be worth it. Don't just project an idea or perception of happiness when you can truly be happy.

Below are chapter summary questions for you to answer.

What are some of the core issues that you struggle with? For example: insecurities, abandonment, trust, feeling worthless, unlovable, not enough, inadequate, etc.

_____
_____
_____
_____
_____

Why these issues?

_____
_____
_____
_____

What do you feel will be the hardest part of being honest with yourself?

_____
_____
_____
_____

Think about the secrets that you are holding onto. Identify how they have impacted your life.

_____
_____
_____
_____

What life adjustments do you need to make as part of your winning journey?

_____
_____
_____
_____

Chapter 7

I'm a Survivor

No storm can last forever.

It will never rain 365 days consecutively.

Keep in mind that trouble comes to pass, not to stay.

Don't worry! No storm, not even the one in your life, can last forever.

~Iyanla Vanzant, Inspirational Speaker

The situations you face in life, no matter how big or small shape your life in some way. Some storms will cause you to feel like giving up is your only option. Winners don't give up. They never quit. You are a winner so you cannot give up. If you are reading this, you have survived 100% of your days. I'd say, those are some great odds you'll survive today too. No matter what you have gone through, you are still here. It didn't physically kill you. Don't let it emotionally murder you either. Know how strong you really are. Your existence is proof of your strength.

We minimize the effect our past experiences have on our present-day life by working through issues in order to remain authentic versions of ourselves. I remember saying to myself, *I'll never be normal.* I said it so much I began to believe it. All of my past experiences have left their mark on me. Some marks are big and some are small. No matter their shape or size, I have learned to embrace them all. My life wasn't always glitter, sparkles and rainbows. Even today I struggle and face obstacles. I could have given up at any moment, but I decided that giving up was not an option.

I was always under the impression that people would never give me the same energy that I have given to them. I was, and am, very much a giving person. The balance came when I saw that giving of myself was more detrimental to me and it was more beneficial to others. I came to understand that not everyone who wants your energy is deserving of it. Your gifts have to be preserved for those who need and deserve them. Not knowing who I was, and giving my energy away, caused me to stay in situations longer than I should have. I am sure you too have stayed in situations, dealing with things that you know you should not have. When my trust in people was broken in early life I internalized that the world was not a safe place. This narrative followed me into adulthood, into relationships, into a marriage and it seeped through to all areas of my life.

The summer before 12th grade my mom reconnected with an old boyfriend and I found out I would be moving 20 miles away. I was upset about the move. This meant a major change. I was disappointed that I would need to leave my friends and teachers behind and transfer my senior year. I was so bummed about the move, but I was excited to see my mom so happy. I only ever wanted my mother to be happy. I had a pattern of spending my life trying to please her, seeking validation, wanting to see and make her smile. The guy she was marrying was a nice man. Still I remember driving down there, feeling sad because I was leaving all my friends. I had been on homecoming court my junior year, and now I was being forced to go to a new school with new people. I didn't make a fuss, or express my true feelings about the move, because if my mom was happy, then I was happy.

I started school and began to adjust, settling in like a typical teenage girl would. Being the outgoing girl, it wasn't hard for me to make friends. I was social. I was a part of various clubs at school. I had a part-time job. My mom ended up being in a car accident after our move so during this time, she didn't work. This gave us more time together. Everything was going okay in my life until the night my mother's husband came into my room.

I had a daybed with a trundle. He would come into my room, lay on the bed and attempt to touch me. With every visit it got harder and harder to push his hands away. I did not want to fight him. I began locking my door.

My mother would yell at me and asked, 'Why are you locking doors around here? You don't pay any bills.' In those days it was a pretty typical parental response. I kept getting into trouble for locking my door so, at some point, I just stopped.

I began to stay at school, helping around campus to avoid going home. I had a boyfriend at the time but I didn't tell a soul. All my friends thought I had the coolest stepdad ever. He would hang out with them and smoke weed with them. However, since I wasn't into drugs or anything like that, I was always an outsider. Little did they know the horror I was living.

He would come in my room a couple of times a week. One night, he told me he was trying to prepare me and teach me what a man should do to a woman. I was disgusted. It reinforced my fear of men. My hyper-vigilance became so severe, that I could not stand to be in any room alone with any man. I kept all of this to myself, continuing to pretend that everything was okay. I side-eyed everyone and was suspicious of everything. When sexual scenes would come on television, I would become very uncomfortable. My mother had no clue. I made sure of it. I didn't tell her, not because I was afraid that she wouldn't believe me, I knew she would have but I didn't want to disrupt her world. I decided not to say anything because my mom had gone through so much and I just wanted her to keep being happy.

I graduated from high school and prepared to go to college. I didn't go away with my friends, as planned, because I felt like I couldn't leave my mom. My mom encouraged me to go chase my dreams. I felt it would be selfish of me to leave her. I think part of that was due to my own co-dependency issues, a fear of being without her.

Now that her life offered time for us to be together the thought of going away to school was less exciting. I wanted to get away from the situation but, when it came time to go, I couldn't make the move. I continued to suffer in silence.

Her husband would give me things, including money, like a bribe for my silence. This was twisted and sick. Looking back, it was predator behavior. When I entered college at 18, everything with him stopped. It had been about two months since he had tried anything. He didn't try me anymore, and I was grateful for that, but the damage lingered. I tried to put it behind me and live as normal a life as possible. Deep down inside, no matter how hard I tried to forget about it, I couldn't.

When Thanksgiving came my mother had planned to travel to New York with my grandmother. That meant I would be alone with him in the house. I think that reality, being alone with him for an extended period, is what caused me to tell my cousin Valencia. 'I have something to tell you, but you have to promise me you won't say anything.' I made her promise, in advance, she would keep my secret. I didn't want to deal with any fallout from telling her what my stepfather had done. Once it came out of my mouth, I immediately wished I hadn't brought it up. At that point, had I not told her, she would have bugged me until I did.

Reluctantly, I confided in her. She said she wouldn't tell anyone. The next day my family gathered at my grandmother's house while she and my mother were away in New York. They questioned me about what was going on. I pretended I didn't know what they were referring to although I was fully aware Valencia had spilled the beans.

When I told them they were of course angry and told me they would not be allowing me to go back to that house. I was partly relieved that I wouldn't have to carry this dark secret anymore. But I was also upset because this meant my life was going to be disrupted again. My job, my school and my life were down south but they wanted me to move immediately. Until my mother returned from New York, I had to stay at my aunt's house. My family told me when mom came back from New York they would sit her down and I had to tell her what had been happening.

I can remember it like it was yesterday. My mom came through my grandmother's door excitedly talking about her trip. My uncle Jeff barely let her get inside before he said, 'We gotta talk.' I was sitting with a sofa pillow over my lap. My mother looked around and asked, 'What's going on?' My family looked at me and said, 'You have to tell her.' Hesitantly I began. Before I could finish mom blurted out 'I'm going to jail.' My family was trying to reason with her, telling her to let the police handle the situation. I was sad, confused, angry at myself for saying anything. Mostly, in a room filled with supportive people, I was alone. I found out later that my cousin told her mom, who in turn told my other aunts and uncles. Looking back, I understand that deep down, I really wanted someone to know.

Telling the Authorities

It was a Monday morning when my mother and I went down to the sheriff's department to make a statement and file a report. They took me into an office and asked me what happened. I told them everything and answered all their questions. The deputy told me my accusations were going to be hard to prove and since I had turned 18, there was nothing that they could do unless the perpetrator admitted their crime. Additionally, they told me that it would be an uphill battle because at this point it was his word against mine. In that moment I left there feeling defeated, like everything I had suffered was for nothing. When it was his turn to speak to the authorities, he told them lies about me. It was very embarrassing and hurtful. Do you know what it feels like to have an adult man, an authority figure, lie on you and make you feel as though what happened was your fault? After all that, nothing ever came of it. Looking back, maybe I could have pursued it more and went through with filing charges, however at 18 years old I did not want that kind of continued distraction in my life. My life had already been altered enough.

Despite my experience I say to you today, if you have been a victim of a crime don't let the possible outcome of the situation prevent you from speaking your truth. After it was over, I still felt as though I wasn't believed. Part of me did wonder what the point of it all was. It left me feeling worse than when it was happening. Being where I am now, I am glad I spoke up. This man was a monster who, thanks to me, was forced to face his internal demons.

After a few months we moved back in the house, along with a close friend of mine. I was comfortable being in the house if I wasn't alone. However, more demons would soon be revealed.

It was also because of my stepdad that I came face-to-face with hardcore drugs. I remember going into the garage one day looking for something. I was opening draws and cabinets and happened to stumble across a white powdery substance that had a razor blade and straw next to it. I slowly closed the cabinet and exited the garage, while thinking to myself *he does real drugs too*. I also kept this to myself until one day I couldn't hold it in. I asked my friend Michelle to come in the garage and look at what I had found. She asked, 'You know what that is, right?' We both agreed that I needed to let my mom know. We took her out to dinner and told her.

By this time, I was still used to keeping secrets. Most of my life had consisted of doing so and it was hard for me to share things about myself or about the things I had experienced. Talking about what I had gone through had made me very uncomfortable and no one ever spoke about it again.

My mom took me to therapy, but I stopped going after about three sessions. In the first session I cried a lot. In the third session I decided I was not going to return. Everything up until this point validated why I could not trust people. Those who were there to protect me could turn and be the ones who hurt me. No one outside of my immediate family knew what had happened to me, not even my friends, and certainly not my father. I kept the mask on. I eventually moved on with my life by becoming actively engaged with campus activities.

Why Me?

I decided to tryout for the basketball cheerleading team at college and I made the team. It was fun. I made a lot of friends on campus, mostly athletes. One evening I attended a campus party. Some of the guys from the university basketball team were there. Music was playing and people seemed to be having fun. One of the guys on the team was on an athletic scholarship from Canada. He asked me to dance. I politely responded, 'No, I'm good.' He proceeded to berate me and became very aggressive with me. I immediately left and felt horrible and confused. I had never, in my life, been attacked that way. I was even more puzzled because I politely said no. I got home and couldn't sleep. I knew I had to sleep because there was a huge championship game the next day. When I woke and got ready the events from the night before were still bothering me. My boyfriend picked me up for the game and could tell, just by the way I was acting, that something was wrong. He questioned me repeatedly, but I refused to tell him because I knew he was a protective guy.

After being bugged to death, I finally gave in and told him what had happened. I begged him not to do anything and hoped very hard that he would listen. He told me he wouldn't do anything crazy and not to worry. I got to campus and went to sit with the rest of the cheerleading team. Most of my friends were on the female basketball team so they were sitting among us. The other team was there and two other teams were on the court playing. Everything was like any other normal game day except the gym was full of visiting teams. As I was sitting with the team, I saw my boyfriend walk in with his entourage. I immediately put my head down. He walked over to me and asked me to show him the guy. I told him no and asked him to leave. He promised me he only wanted to talk to him. The next thing I knew almost everyone on the team was fighting. I was mortified. I already didn't like confrontation, now all of this was transpiring because of me.

One of the guys from our team, someone I had considered a friend until that moment began to walk towards me very aggressively. He pointed and yelled, 'This is all your fault!' He picked me up by my neck and slammed me on the gym floor. Someone grabbed him. If they hadn't, he would have fought me as if he was fighting another man. My friends who were watching the entire episode unfold helped me up. Prior to the assault, my boyfriend and his entourage ran off because the campus police arrived on the scene. I can remember the team on the court stopping the game to watch the chaos unfold. It was so violent that the school's large trophy case ended up smashed- glass was everywhere. Someone contacted my mother and she arrived at the gym as soon as she could. I was transported to the hospital and told by the attending physician I had a sprained neck and a concussion. I couldn't believe what had happened

Once I left the hospital, I worried about the damage all of this had caused. The torture wasn't over just yet. When I arrived at school the following Monday I was asked to stop by the athletic director's office, who also happened to be the basketball coach. He asked me to turn in my uniform and I was dismissed from the cheerleading squad. I was also informed that since the player who had verbally assaulted me was on a school visa, and attending school on a scholarship, he was expelled from school and deported back to Canada. I felt horrible about the entire situation.

That same day I attempted to go into the student union. I did this every day, but this day I was immediately attacked by the men's basketball team. They blamed me for the team having to forfeit the championship and for their teammate being deported. They angrily expressed they had every intention of making my life a living hell. To this very day, I have never stepped foot back into that gym or the student union.

My mother was aware of the threats being made towards me. She suggested we take the advice of the hospital and go down to the courthouse to get an order of protection. We took a day and drove down to the courthouse, intent on leaving with that order. That's not what happened. I ended up being told that since the guy who sprained my neck was not an intimate partner, they could not grant an order of protection because my report did not meet the guidelines. I left there, once again, feeling defeated. A few days later I was told that the guy who had physically assaulted me had also been expelled and sent back to Ohio after losing his basketball scholarship. This only made me feel worse.

Looking back now, I'm glad I wasn't blamed by the school and expelled as well. After that my life on campus was comprised of mad dashes to my classes. I kept a very low profile and kept to myself. Luckily for me, I only had a few semesters left before graduation. I dropped out of all campus activities and stayed away from any location I thought team players would be. The entire experience was miserable. I was afraid. I was unhappy. I was depressed. Despite everything I was going through, I still managed to hide my feelings. This situation again validated why I should have kept my mouth closed. It seemed as though any time I opened my mouth to share my feelings, or speak my truth, I came away more devastated.

Throughout all of these experiences the same underlying themes began to emerge. As the winner in you continues to develop, you will have to be mindful of the common unhealthy themes that will need to be worked through and addressed. A few of the common themes that stuck out for me were always feeling unsafe, a lack of security and always running. I ran away from my issues rather than face them. I ran away from who I was by not acknowledging the real me.

I eventually moved on, transferring to Nova Southeastern University. By this time, I had a new boyfriend and was working 30 hours a week while going to school full-time. I was driving over an hour with traffic for classes and working in the evenings. It was September of 2004, when I noticed a lump in my neck. I walked into class shortly after and asked a few classmates if they saw what I saw. They all agreed that something was there. This strange lump had suddenly appeared out of nowhere. Before that day, I had never noticed it. When I got home, I showed my mom and she suggested I go have it checked out. I called the doctor and made an appointment. The doctor checked it out and told me that, because my life was so busy, it was stress in my body manifesting itself physically. She prescribed an anti-inflammatory and sent me on my way.

In February of 2005, my boyfriend proposed. After graduation, I was offered a job and was slated to start the 1st of September. I was so excited because this was going to be my first real job. My life was going along swell. 2005 was shaping up to be an amazing year for me.

A week after accepting the job, I began to have pain in that same area of my neck. I checked into the emergency room and, after tests, was informed that I had an infection in my lymphatic system. It was strongly recommended that I have it checked out. Not thinking anything of it, I made an appointment. During my next appointment with the doctor, her assistant told me that the doctor would be referring me to an ear, nose and throat (ENT) specialist, because she had done everything for me that she could.

I saw the ENT the following week. Every test he ordered came back negative. On my last visit he told me he wanted me to do a biopsy. He scheduled an oncology consult. I was baffled at the idea of having an oncology appointment when everything was coming back negative and normal. The doctor assured me that it was just protocol. My biopsy was scheduled for a Tuesday and my oncology visit was scheduled for the Monday following the biopsy. I had the biopsy and I heard nothing. In my mind, no news meant good news.

The Friday after my biopsy, sitting in Macys with my fiancé picking out gift registry items, I received a call from my mother. The doctor was also on the call and needed my permission to speak to her. Questions were running through my mind but, being young and in love, I was mostly really annoyed that I was dealing with this while I was trying to select gifts for my registry. I agreed to the phone conversation and was sure that everything was fine since he was willing to give my results by phone. 'Looking at your chart,' he said, 'I do see that your results came back positive for Lymphoma. I also see it noted that you have an appointment with the oncologist on Monday.' He asked if I had any questions. I responded as if everything was fine. I kept my composure and smiled at the lady helping us with the registry as I put my finger up indicating to her that I needed just a few more moments.

After hearing my mom breakdown, and drop the phone, I got off the call and turned to my fiancé. I told him we needed to go then looked at the attendant and told her that I would need to reschedule the appointment. I remember the car ride home was silent.

The only person I called was my best friend at the time. She told me that she would meet me at my house. I can remember feeling like I needed to be strong for my mother. Here I was again, ignoring my own feelings and worrying about everyone else. I got home, still in shock and disbelief. I spent that entire weekend confused and numb. I didn't really cry because I didn't want to seem weak. I didn't want my mom to worry about me.

Monday came and I went to my oncology appointment. I had a bone marrow biopsy done and surgery was scheduled for the following Wednesday. My lymph nodes were removed and a port placement was installed in preparation for chemotherapy. I was scheduled for my first chemo treatment that Friday. Thursday of that same week I was slated to start my new job. I received the biopsy of my neck on the 23rd of August. I was diagnosed on the 26th of August. I had my bone biopsy on the 29th of August. I had surgery and my port placed on the 30th of August. I started my new job on the 1st of September and had my first chemotherapy session on the 2nd of September. Everything was happening so fast. I didn't even have time to breathe, let alone think about how I really felt.

The day after my surgery I was to report for my first day of work. It was going to be my first real job, a job in my field. How could I call in on my first day? Remember how my mind worked. I thought I had to be superwoman and prove myself to people. I was advised not to report to work due to the medications I was on. I told my mom I wouldn't take my pain medications and that I needed to show up for my first day. When Wednesday came, I drove slowly and made it to work on time. I looked like hell! I walked into Human Resources and completed my paperwork. I took my company photo, which I still have to this day. It looks horrible but I did what I felt I needed to do. After all the employee forms were filled out, I explained to the Human Resources director what was going on. She told me that I would need to speak to the program director. I was so afraid. Surely, I was going to be fired on the spot, I thought. The physical pain I was in was overshadowed by my anxiety.

I walked into the director's office and proceeded to tell her what was going on. She listened and didn't say a word until I was finished. I nervously looked around just waiting for her to tell me they no longer needed my services. To my surprise she shared that she was a two-time cancer survivor and she understood. She gave me the rest of the day off and told me to go prepare for surgery and that she'd see me on Monday. I was so thankful and relieved. I couldn't believe that I still had the job. I took this experience as God's way of saying to me 'I've got your back, just as I always have.'

My cancer journey was an ugly one. It was painful, debilitating and physically scarring. Outside of the severe physical pain associated with treatments, and the side effects, there was only one real time that I cried. The first time I cried about my battle with cancer was when I sat to have my first chemo. I was sitting in the chair eating souse (*Caribbean broth*) and watching a talk show. I looked up at the bags of medication flowing through me and began to realize that this was my new normal. As tears fell to my cheeks, I questioned my own mortality.

Just as I had always done in the past, I separated me, as an individual, from what I was going through. This was not a good thing. Although it allowed me to have a positive outlook, and believe that I was going to make it, I never really dealt with my true feelings about being diagnosed with cancer. Because I felt I had to be strong, I never processed how I truly felt about anything that had ever happened in my life. I had to learn that winners take the time to notice how they are feeling, what they are feeling, and allow themselves to feel it throughout their body. I was so used to suppressing and ignoring everything that I began to disconnect from my physical self. On the outside it presented as strength. It was part intellectualization and part rationalization.

Even as a therapist, I never took the time to really think about my feelings. I was so used to having to be strong that being strong became my biggest enemy. The notion of having to be strong was serving no purpose in my life. I was not addressing the real issues. I got through everything and survived, but the residual effects of the situations I experienced continued to linger.

Being a winner and overcoming is not just about surviving. You must be in a place where you can heal as well. You can't be a broken winner. My life was fragmented. My only coping skill was to push myself harder. I worked every day. When it was time for me to get radiation treatments, I would go during my lunch break and then return to work. Looking back, I was insane. I didn't allow myself time to think, about anything. In the end, I survived all these situations. There were so many more that were to come and I survived them too. I wore my pain like a badge of honor. I was okay sharing that part of me because, in my mind, it made me stronger. No one was able to question my strength, or my ability to overcome. I felt like that I was enough for me, or at least I did in the moment.

After going through years of pain, hurt and betrayal my untrusting view of people was intensified. I expected people to fail me. More than one person I'd trusted to protect me in my life let me down. This caused my faith in people to diminish. I found myself questioning my own ability to read and judge people's motives and intentions. I trusted less and was cautious of who I let into my life. It continued to shape my view of the world. I entered every situation highly suspicious of others. My suspicions of others, and mistrust of the world, never impacted how much I continued to give of myself. I began to expect negative things, such as the things that had happened to me, to continue happening.

When people would try to get close to me, I would keep them at arm's length. Because I was, and am, an extravert no one ever suspected my internal conflict. I loved being around people, I just didn't trust them. Today my infectious smile and laugh are, thankfully, an authentic reflection of where I am in life. Despite going through everything I've endured, two things I never lost were my smile and my giving heart.

Below are chapter summary questions for you to answer.

Reflect on your life and list times you've wanted to give up but found the courage to not just survive but overcome.

_____
_____
_____
_____

What are some of the things that prevented you from giving up?

_____
_____
_____
_____

How does your current life reflect winning beyond mere survival?

_____
_____
_____
_____

List at least five (5) things you can do to prevent yourself from becoming jaded as a result of past experiences.

_____
_____
_____
_____

Identify two (2) things that you are embarrassed to reveal out of fear of being judged.

_____
_____
_____
_____

Chapter 8

Learning to Let Go and Allowing God to Have Full Control

There is never a moment when God is not in control.

Relax! He's got you covered.

~ Mandy Hale, The Single Woman: Life, Love, and a Dash of Sass

I moved to Central Florida after being offered a clinical director position at an inpatient substance abuse facility. This gave me the opportunity to grow as a professional because I had never experienced an inpatient facility. All of my knowledge was based in outpatient settings. I was nervous but excited about the move. I trusted that I was making the right decision. I packed up and moved my daughter and I to Orlando. After being at the facility for a little over two years, I accepted another position as the clinical director of a different facility. It was very far from where I lived but the company made it worth my while.

This would be the fifth start-up program developed with my assistance. This was also the program I had the most creative control over. Every document and policy was created, and implemented, by me. I gave everything to making sure that the clinical infrastructure of the program was stellar.

There came a period in time when talk of an acquisition became a reality. Another administrator and I were in close talks with the new company and were assured that we would be coming over once the acquisition was final. I was a little worried because I know how these things can go. I never thought however, that I would be sitting at the other side of the table hearing that I would no longer be a part of the organization. I had spent the last two years developing their model and now they didn't want me to run it. I did not know how to feel. I never saw it coming. They told me that I didn't fit the leadership culture. I was really hurt, shocked and confused. I felt like I didn't have any closure because they could not give me specific examples for their reasoning.

When I lost my job my faith was tested. My life had changed in an instant. I began to wonder how I would take care of my daughter and pay our bills. I had to face the reality that I was trusting more in my own human abilities than I was in God. I knew that He had always been my source, but I struggled with being in the space of the unknown. I had been tested before but now I needed to withstand the thing I feared the most. It has been a journey, but I have been able to let go and trust that God has complete control over my life.

I didn't allow myself to worry too much. How could I say I trusted God if, in the same breath, I expressed worry and stress? Why would I worry about the things that God had already worked out?

My last day on my job was a Tuesday. On Wednesday I was offered a new position. I had to be mindful of how I looked at this offer. It wasn't the hours I needed. It wasn't a position that I was used to having. My leadership and creative abilities would not be utilized. I wasn't making the amount of money that I was used to making. I was so used to being in a position of leadership that I categorized the new position as a layover until I could find something I really wanted. Considering all these factors, I asked, *'Is this you God?'*

It wasn't until I had been in my new job a few weeks that I realized the position was allowing me to do everything I had been wanting. The job was less stressful and I had more time available to spend with my daughter and family. I could begin to enjoy life.

Before I received the offer I prayed that I would secure a high executive position with great pay and benefits. Those doors didn't open and it caused me to reevaluate if I was ignoring the blessing I had received. I had overlooked how this new position addressed all my needs. I was so busy expecting God to answer my prayers the way I wanted him to, that I couldn't see He had answered my prayers the way they needed to be answered. I was right where He wanted me to be, right where I needed to be. I realized that I had been ungrateful for the blessing I had been given.

Because I had experienced so many shocking life situations I felt things were often outside of my control and the things I could control became that much more important to me. No one could tell me anything. I wanted to do things my way. I didn't want, or need, anyone's input. I constantly found myself running into roadblocks, often dead-ended by this mentality.

If control is one of the things you struggle with you are not alone. I believe most people like to know what's going to happen in their lives. We have one, three and five-year plans for our expectations of life. It's important for you to dream, but realize too that you can't dictate how every step of the way will play out. You can't control the pieces to the puzzle. If this is an area you struggle in you should ask yourself why you feel the need to control everyone/thing around you. Whether you know it or not fear is usually at the root of control. Although you may be telling yourself you have faith, the reality is you really have fear.

Have Faith

I needed to learn that having control did not equate to success. It did, however, equate to increased levels of stress. Once you learn about, and get to know, your true self having to prove yourself to others goes away. Because of the many times I'd been let down and betrayed, I had a hard time placing my future in someone else's hands. At times that included

God's. In my mind I knew that God was the answer, but I doubted him. My emotions and actions were proof of that doubt. How could I think that I knew better than my Creator, what was in my best interest? I didn't want to lean on Him to guide me because I was so afraid of letting go of my perceived control. I had to learn that winners take suggestions. I truly became a winner when I relaxed into the fact that God has everything under control.

I remember wondering if He still heard me when I prayed. I wanted reassurance. A receipt from heaven confirming that God heard my prayers would have been great! Because of my untrusting view of the world I needed that security, a guarantee that I wouldn't be left alone. I came to realize that not having that certainty is faith. I didn't have to have reassurance about the things that worried me. I believed in the One that would work it all out. This was such a hard concept to put into practice. I understood it, but it took a while for me to totally operate under the premise.

At the time I was diagnosed with cancer, I felt like my purpose had not been fulfilled, that I wouldn't be able to share my story with others. Although I was scared, and it was painful, I believed and trusted in God. I had faith but it wasn't consistent faith. My faith fluctuated.

While you are trusting God, and operating in faith, your trust in God can't be shaken. I had to internalize that believing in him was more than just words. My ability to trust and believe God's word had to be backed by action. What was I doing to indicate my trust in God? Was I praying about things I would then try to fix on my own?

As I began to develop as a winner it was a challenge to resolve the notion to keep holding on. I found myself second-guessing my actions. This came from not knowing my true self. I had to remind myself that God had never failed me. Even though unfortunate things happened in my life they never ended me. I was used to second-guessing things, expecting things to go wrong. By continuing to do this, I invited negative things into my life.

Once you begin to operate in faith, pay attention not to operate with a sense of false faith. False faith is saying you trust and believe in God but you act differently. False faith hangs onto control. False faith is saying you trust but secretly you are in fear things will not work out for you. Not being sure it was God validated my need to maintain control of a situation. I used God as an excuse.

When you trust God, you trust that everything will be okay. This allows you to release control. You can't say you trust Him to control the situation if you are trying to dictate the narrative. It's your story but He has the outline. You're writing the content.

Earlier in my life I can recall a time when I was ill that caused me to be confused as to why this was happening to me. When things happened in my life, I wanted to know the why of it. I wasn't yet able to allow things to flow freely, to continually trust Him. I needed to learn that it was okay for me to release, and trust in his ability. I needed to know that God would direct me and that he had blessed me with a thing called intuition.

Due to my complicated health history my pregnancy was high-risk. During labor they could not find my daughter's heartbeat. I was in excruciating pain. When I saw the looks on the nurses faces I knew something was wrong. I had an emergency C-section. I remember my mother telling me the doctor came out at one point to tell her, he thought he may need to ask her which one of us to save. That is a very scary thing to hear. I needed to let go of my fears and trust that God had blessed me with a medical team that was capable of doing everything necessary for me to have a successful delivery.

Trusting your Intuition

In January of 2007, I tried, but was unable, to pick up my newborn daughter. My husband thought I was being a drama queen, but I was in serious pain. Something inside told me something was seriously wrong. I contacted the doctor's office and an appointment was made. The next day my doctor ordered imaging of my veins. Due to the number of people coming in the room during the procedure I thought something was wrong. They told me I was all set and my doctor would be contacting me with the results. My doctor called before I made it home. He told me to go straight to the hospital. I met my doctor at the hospital and was admitted before being informed that I had a blood clot in my jugular.

Thank God I listened to the voice inside and not the people around me. When we are in tune with ourselves, it allows us to be more in tune with, and listen to, our bodies. After being in the hospital for three days I was released. I spent the next nine months giving myself anticlotting medication injections. By listening to my God-given intuition, my life had been saved. I was able to trust the voice within and get the help I needed. He gave me the ability to listen to my inner voice and act.

Over time I began to notice that every time I worried, stressed and became overwhelmed by things, God had already provided the answer. He was consistent. Even though the answer may not have come in the form I wanted, I was always provided a solution. I would say, *I want to hear from God* without realizing everything he was showing me. A still small voice would always speak to me and direct my path.

Trusting my God-given intuition, listening to my gut, being faithful and relinquishing control to God was the only way I could ever become a successful winner. Once I gave the control over to him, I could leave it with him. Like a child riding a bike with training wheels that's where my faith was. I would need to take the training wheels off and have full unshakeable faith that God had everything under control.

Despite whatever you may have gone through in life, you must get to a place where it doesn't cloud your future. Don't allow your shortcomings, or the mistakes you've made to derail you from destiny. Look to the future, have faith and trust that God will not fail you. With God by your side you will win and you will be successful. Believe that better is coming and better will arrive.

Just because you allow God to have control doesn't mean you stop working. It doesn't mean that you wait for God to do it all. Letting go and allowing God to have control means that you don't get caught up in what the circumstances may look like. God is in the driver's seat, but you need to navigate your path. Faith without work is dead- *James 2:17*. Have faith that God will do what is needed but show him that you are willing to share the workload.

If you want to be a winner, you are going to have to take your hands off situations and allow God to have control. In some form or fashion we all want to, to a large extent, be in control of our lives. Being in control becomes an issue when we begin to get in our own way. Some of us feel so out of control that the only way to resolve this is by hyper-controlling certain areas. When you have a deep need to control things the driving force of that need usually comes from fear.

You might have a fear of failing, not producing, not being good enough, or not achieving which comes from someplace deeper inside. You may think that having full control of everything around you makes you strong but it really showcases your weaknesses. Having total control is an illusion. There is no way to guarantee perfection. You are human, which means you are vulnerable. You don't have control over external factors, especially other people. The tighter you hold onto a thing the more you suffocate it and, eventually, you'll lose it. When you hold on tight to the things you are trying to control you lose control of yourself.

What is controlling your life, faith or fear? I have learned so much over the years regarding trust and control. Take time to identify the things in your life that may need adjusting. Practice this daily. Take your hands out of situations and let go. Why are you trying to control things that are outside of your control anyway? Have faith and trust in the fact that He will provide.

Winners do things that are hard. If letting go has been a challenge for you, then you are on the right track. Winners have matured to a level that allows them to see the possibility in a thing more than the thing itself. This simply means the winner is not focused on the problem but is more focused on the solution. As a winner trust yourself, and your ability to trust in God.

We can get to a place where we are in our own way. When God blesses you, the blessing may not look the way you imagined. Had He given me what I had been praying for, I would not have been able to do the things I needed to do. Had I controlled the situation, I would not have been able to see the benefits of His plan. God knew what I needed better than I did. That was enough to reinforce my faith and renew my trust in God's plan for my life.

Winners know when to let go. They know releasing control is not a reflection of weakness. I no longer needed validation through a position or title. This is only because I was able to spend time getting to know myself. That was time granted through loosing my mask of self. I now understand who I am as the person outside of my achievements. I learned fast that the reason doors to the corporate world were closed to me was because God was taking me to a different level, a place where I wouldn't need to work for anyone unless I wanted to.

Winners know who they are. They have taken the time to get to know themselves. The more you know who you are, the more your developing winner will win. When you find yourself stressing take a deep breath, relax and know that God has you. I know it won't be easy at first, but it can be done. As you begin to see yourself as a winner use all the concepts of this guide to help you move toward operating with a winning mindset. Winners know how to take suggestions. They don't give up when things don't appear to be the way they would like for them to be.

Below are chapter summary questions for you to answer.

What concepts stood out for you as you read this chapter?

_____
_____
_____
_____

What causes you to fear releasing control?

_____
_____
_____
_____

What are the things that prevent you from trusting in God and giving him control?

_____
_____
_____
_____

Identify things you will do to assist moving past those barriers, addressed in the question above.

_____
_____
_____
_____

Chapter 9

Overcoming: The Rebirthing of a Winner

"Your strength doesn't come from winning. It comes from struggles and hardship. Everything that you go through prepares you for the next level."

~ Germany Kent, Journalist

Shedding the part of me that was full of shame, pain and fear was cathartic. I really got to know myself during the process. I had to cut some people out of my life. I had to do some deep inner work. When you need time for you, be sure that you take it. People around you may get upset or may not understand what you are doing, but that is okay. If they get mad at you for bettering yourself, then they might not truly have your best interests at heart.

Some elevations in your life are going to require isolation. Learn to be okay alone with yourself. In order to get to know the real you, you are going to have to spend time alone. Don't allow people to make you feel bad for protecting your peace. Take time outs. I, oftentimes, felt a sense of obligation to explain my behavior or needs. I had to wake up and realize I'm not obligated, nor should I feel obligated, to explain anything to anyone when it comes to my personal peace, and the decisions I make regarding it. Healing and protecting your peace is about no one but you. If they can't respect your boundaries, then they don't respect you.

When it comes to boundaries, you must make sure that they are clearly defined and effectively communicated. People in your life are not mind readers. You cannot expect them to automatically know when you create a new boundary. The more consistent you are with enforcing your boundaries, the more people will respect them. You can't in one breath say, "I'm not allowing negative energy in my space," then the next minute you're the person spreading gossip about others. That is sending mixed messages, a sure indicator that you are not respecting your boundaries- so they don't have to either. If you spend everyday walking in your truth, people won't have any trouble figuring out who you are. Winners walk in their truths. They know that they are representing authentic versions of themselves.

Stop hiding and start living. If you are hiding behind a mask or are pretending to be something you aren't because you don't know who you are- you are not living.

Who are you on the inside?

What makes you, you?

What are your ambitions and passions?

What are your imperfectly perfect flaws?

Winners don't give up. They take time to acknowledge their true feelings. Winners don't stay down. They evaluate and learn from past situations. Winners don't whine. They take time to nurture their emotions.

Do the work you need to do in your life, even if that means getting rid of toxic people or things. There are some things that you won't be able to achieve if you allow negative energy to stay in your life. As discussed, the first E of the E.F.F.E.C.T. model is evaluate and elevate. Think about the things holding you back and let them go.

I survived death, on more than one occasion, and it's something I have learned to be thankful for. I see that my being a winner was more than just surviving.

Not many people talk about the ugly side of surviving. Behind every winner, there's a survivor who had to overcome many obstacles and challenges. I've survived so many things in my life. I can say I'm prouder now, because I didn't just survive them. I'm thriving and winning.

Situations that could have easily taken me out, didn't. Throughout my journey to becoming a winner, I had to tweak my definition of the word survivor. Surviving no longer means just getting through it. It now means not allowing the situation to keep me bound.

Winners are free to live in their truth, free to walk in their purpose, and free to forgive themselves for not loving themselves enough before. I was able to survive, overcome and become a winner. I'm here to tell you, you can do the same. Don't allow past experiences, or hard feelings, to hold you back. Like all the people who hurt me, I too was covered in self-deception. I didn't know the real version of myself. Winners know who they are and take their rightful places in life. When we are not honest with who we are, we allow the masks we created to define us.

As a winner, don't bring old ways of thinking into your future. Winners are honest with themselves and that's how they continue to survive. Life will not always be easy. Be the kind of winner who takes time to heal their past and leave it there.

Winners know how to survive even the toughest situations and not become jaded in the process. In the book *Masters of Success*, legendary Packers coach Vince Lombardi wrote, "The successful man is himself. To be successful, you've got to be honest with yourself." When you begin to live and speak your truth, you have the power to be more successful and not just survive, but win.

You have overcome many obstacles and you are still standing. Many things you have experienced were the same things that other people didn't survive. Now what? Where do you go from here? Once you experience trials, hard times and obstacles, how do you begin to take the necessary steps to move forward with your life? I have to admit it can be very difficult picking yourself up off the ground. Not everyone overcomes tough situations. As you become a winner, you will not only be getting up and dusting off, you'll be unable to be kept down.

You will need to work every day to adjust your perception of situations that come your way. As a winner defeat becomes foreign to you. Winners don't start, only to stop. Winners keep going, no matter how the situation changes. When something becomes difficult, push through it, think positive and know that you are stronger than whatever you're facing. If we begin to tell ourselves that we won't be able to overcome a situation, then guess what, we won't. If we instead tell ourselves we can overcome, the likelihood of success increases exponentially. You must have faith in your abilities to achieve greatness.

Be cautious not to talk yourself into a negative mindset that keeps you trapped. Remember your strength does not come from winning; it comes from you being able to overcome the struggles and hardships that life throws your way. Winners learn and grow from every situation they encounter, good or bad. If you find yourself unable to learn from a situation, I suggest you conduct a self-check and assess if you are still holding on to regret, doubt, resentment or bitterness.

When we continue to hold onto the past, we take up space that could better serve more positive purposes. See your life as a jar. The jar can only hold so much. If you fill the jar with things that are negative, you won't have room for the positive. The more negative, the harder it will be for you to see, and accept, anything positive.

Maybe you're saying, 'Okay I've overcome, now what?' The next phase is maintenance. Being able to maintain what you have accomplished is the winner's- "What Now." You must continue to overcome every day. Every day there are new challenges placed in your life. Winners aren't always on top of the world. They understand that there will be days that they barely make it through. Giving up is never an option in the mind of a winner because the winner understands that there is no endgame to winning.

In the life of a winner, the mark is consistently being adjusted to make room for new goals when old ones are achieved. Winning is a continuum, a mindset. The things we have overcome only help to prepare for the next levels in our lives. In every situation there are lessons to be learned.

Everyone Makes Mistakes

Winners learn from past mistakes so that they don't repeat them. When a winner does repeat a mistake, they reflect on the lessons in an effort to avoid further repetition.

A winner also takes what they have learned and shares it with others. Sharing how you were able to overcome is a practice commonly used by winners. When a winner can relate to others experiencing the same challenges it is a moment of growth for all involved. A winner who is able to share what they've learned is a mentor indeed.

If you are having a hard time helping others, or are in a space where you don't want to see others win, you have more work to do before you can become a winner. The importance of working through the W.O.W. Effect includes having a solid perception of who you are as a winner. If you are secure in yourself, and your abilities, then seeing others win will be rewarding for you. If you still feel the need to compete with others, you aren't there yet. Winners have too much going on in their own lives to worry about other people's goals. Winning is not always easy. Winners don't just breeze through every situation unscathed. There are times when winners will want to weep. Winners don't indulge whining. They process and proceed.

As you begin to live as a winner, you need to recognize that there will be times when you'll get tired and want to give up. It's okay to be tired. It's not okay to quit. GIVING UP IS NOT AN OPTION. Yes, you read that correctly, I'm yelling. There is too much riding on your ability to keep going to say it politely. Just look at how far you've already come, and imagine the greatness you'll achieve, by following the W.O.W. E.F.F.E.C.T. model.

There will be hurdles placed in front of you J.U.M.P. The J.U.M.P. model is how we overcome hurdles or obstacles that appear in our lives. This concept should be an easy one to remember. When an obstacle comes your way be ready to J.U.M.P.! Review the following model and be ready to J.U.M.P. over your next obstacle with ease.

(J) = Judiciously Evaluate

When situations arise in your life, as a winner, you will need to have a clear mind to respectfully evaluate what you are facing. Take the necessary time to evaluate a situation. We often get caught up in the fluff that surrounds a situation and we lose focus. The actual issue is your only problem to solve. Do that and everything else will fall into its rightful place. Stay focused. Evaluate the obstacles and devise a plan.

(U) = Understand Your Position

When you understand your position related to the issue, you are better able to make decisions. Decisions rooted in understanding are based on facts, not feelings. It will be impossible to make a rational decision, a decision that is in your best interest, if you don't know where you stand on an issue. Be clear about who you are and what you want for a resolution. Don't allow your feelings surrounding the situation to influence your judgment when it comes to handling the issue.

(M) = Make a Plan

When you prepare from a place of understanding you are mindful of your position, the obstacle and your needs. That data can inform your decisions moving forward, your plan, regardless of fears. Planning includes making sure you have backup ideas in place in case of failure.

Thinking about the worse possible outcome before it happens puts you in a great space. Not only do you have safeguards in place you'll know how to counter the other side's position because you've considered it. Best of all, getting the what ifs out of the way early on in the process, and making a plan that accommodates or overcomes them, helps fear, negativity and pessimism subside.

When the worse case scenario does happen, its no longer tragic because you already have a plan in place to overcome it. Because you've previously considered it, you've been through the emotion of it so it hits with less pain, allowing you to bounce back quicker. Knowing you have developed a plan outlining your goal will quell the inner pessimist and calm your nerves too.

(P) = Prepare for Your Win

Prepare yourself to win with positive thinking. This is very necessary for a winner. Even if the situation does not turn out the way you planned, you are able to make it through, you have won. Winning encompasses surviving, thriving and realizing the strength you have within. Winners don't quit. They keep pressing forward. They overcome so they can win in life.

Now that you know how to J.U.M.P. without hurting yourself you can identify experiences where you've used the J.U.M.P. model. There are likely numerous examples of your jumping capabilities. Any decisions made without emotion generally follow the model. Once you begin to use the J.U.M.P. model to push through your emotional barriers you'll be chanting, "iWin, iWon, iWOW." This (iWin, iWon, iWOW) is a personal mantra I created as a reminder that I can win, I have won, and I can wow and overcome anything placed in my path.

You've pushed over an emotional wall and are still here to talk about it. It doesn't stop there but it is a great place to reflect on your progress, reward yourself with a bit of gratitude and then, prepare to roll up your sleeves. Winning is not going to be glitter, sparkles and rainbows. Winning is hard work. You will only get out of it precisely what you are willing to put into it. If you don't put in your total effort, that will be your result. People only half-do anything because they weren't committed to it in the first place.

If the thing you have to do is a plan B or a compromise, step up. You're only in a position to need compromise because you've approached it from a spot of vulnerability.

How dedicated are you to the winning process when you are faced with tough situations you have to overcome? Giving up is an easy, but destructive alternative. As you develop your winning mindset, it will become harder for you to give up. That's when you'll know winning is now a part of who you are. When you win, you will get dirty, and some situations may get stinky, but the winner is built for exactly these situations.

A Clearer View

Once the journey becomes clear, you can focus your attention. Distractions will come into your life but you'll be able to remain focused, and on target. Winners have a proven track record for overcoming tough situations.

How do you know when you've entered the winning stage of your life? For starters, winners have gone through experiences that have tested their winning spirit. There is not a single winner on this planet that hasn't been through a tough situation. If you haven't gone through anything how are you be able to learn and hone your ability for overcoming situations? The winner in you must be tested.

How you operate under pressure is a telltale sign of your progression toward winning. Even when a winner gets off track, they can regain focus. Maintaining focus should become an everyday habit that you practice. For example, if you identify a goal, and that goal no longer serves a purpose, you will need to reevaluate and refocus. Adjust to completed goals is also something that may be a challenge to overcome.

If you picked up this book in hopes of achieving a long-standing goal, and now you've reached that marker, you can feel a sense of finality. While it is important to celebrate milestones, you should also be planning for what comes next. This is how to operate with a winning mindset and ensure the goal you worked so hard to accomplish remains worthy of the sacrifices and efforts you put into achieving it. Regularly reviewing and adjusting goals will keep you developing as a winner.

Becoming complacent is a sure way to undo or stop any progression that has taken place. When you are complacent, you no longer see the need to evaluate. Lack of evaluation holds you hostage, it immobilizes you, keeping you from moving forward on your journey.

The winner also benefits, and stays focused, by utilizing the traffic light in their lives. Remember green is for go or execution, yellow is for caution or evaluation, and red is for stop or plan. When a winner is in the green, they can cruise along with no worries or distractions as they execute a plan. They deal with situations with limited help or distractions. If distractions do appear, they are minor, and pose no threat to the end goal.

When the winner is operating in the yellow, this means that they are comfortable. This is the reflection and celebration mode. They evaluate what is going on with the situation, processing to see if there are any alternative routes that need to be taken.

When a winner is operating in the red, they are stopped. They are complacent, in place, when they should be planning their next move. This is where a previously identified goal may be aborted.

I was not always this put together. I remember obsessing over all the mistakes I'd made. I would fret so much I became physically ill. I had panic attacks that scared the living crap out of me. This was clearly not needed as a cherry on top of the health challenges I was already facing. I told myself, over and over, I had failed. I was very unhealthy. Had I known then what I know now I would not have spent so much time obsessing. You live and learn; I'd like to think better late than never. Because I was able to learn the hard truths about becoming a winner, I am now able to accomplish my goal of becoming a writer because I have the knowledge to share tools, concepts and techniques I developed on my winning path.

Get to a place where you are no longer developing yourself into a winner but maintaining the winner you are. Just like a great weight loss or sobriety plan, once you are able to operate in a winning mindset, you will need to maintain. You maintain by continually practicing habits that lead to your success. This is the difference between winning and having won.

Winning is an ever-changing journey, not a destination. Take the time to get to know yourself. Stand in, and for, your truth. Be able to say I know who I am is one of the most freeing and satisfying feelings a person could ever experience. Everything you seek will fall into place once you embrace your journey. Be the winner you and I both know you can be.

Winners don't get complacent or lose site on where they are going. They are active in their ability to progress. They know that in order to maintain their winning mindset, they must make decisions in alignment with being a winner. Having done all of these things, you will have a renewed sense of who you are as a winner. Winners do the work and train so that they can J.U.M.P. whenever necessary. Prepare yourself to J.U.M.P. when needed. Winners always stay prepared. Are you prepared for your win?

Below are chapter summary questions for you to answer.

Identify areas in your life that demonstrate a time when you overcame an obstacle.

_____
_____
_____
_____

What will you need to overcome a current obstacle?

_____
_____
_____
_____

How is that obstacle impacting your life?

_____
_____
_____
_____

What behaviors do you regularly practice that demonstrate your ability to overcome this obstacle?

_____
_____
_____
_____

How will you prepare to overcome the obstacle?

_____
_____
_____
_____

What will you do if you are unable to achieve your end-goal as it relates to this obstacle?

_____
_____
_____
_____

Chapter 10

The Superhero vs. the Villain Within

"You can either be a victim of the world or an adventurer in search of treasure. It all depends on how you view your life."

~Paulo Coelho, Eleven Minutes

Who is your favorite superhero? Strange question I know but think about it for a moment. Did you think of yourself when you pictured the superhero? I'm sure you didn't. Most times when we think about a superhero, we think of a superhuman figure that transcends natural laws elements and gravity; someone that fights crime and the evil villain. But what if I told you, you are a superhero? Would you believe me?

It's my theory that we all have a superhero inside of us, it's what keeps us fighting and winning against the things that come our way. What amazes me is how we understate our own power.

As we begin to operate with a winning mindset, we need to see ourselves as winners with the strength of a superhero. This does not mean we are picking up buildings and saving the world from evil villains. This does mean we've tapped into our ability to think like a champion. Winners are champions because they have the power to J.U.M.P. over the obstacles that appear in their lives. Every one of us has a superhero inside. We can accomplish things that we never thought possible if we let our inner hero take action. The superhero within operates with a winning mentality.

Identifying the Villain in your Life

Your inner villain uses fear and trauma to keep you safe from the harms that sometimes come from the risks necessary for a winning life. Just as they do in the comic books, these mindsets compete for your attention. When their battle becomes overwhelming remember – the path to winning is paved by action. Your inner villain's job is to stifle growth and encourage stagnation. Your inner hero motivates you to act.

As you become a winner and maintain your winner status, you will need to remain mindful of how you deal with, and process, new challenges. When your villain is the lead you will own your part in the situation. Self-preservation has you playing the blame game, whining loudest to be heard over your own shortcomings. Don't squeaky wheel your life. When the volume is equalized, will your story hold water? Villains don't learn, they react. They expect everything to be handled outside of their realm, which makes sense because the villain only exists to protect you from a real or imagined invasion.

Winners understand the hard work and dedication it takes to become, and maintain, their superhero status. They know that being the best version of themselves is enough to be rewarded and that being the best is a continuous learning and training process. They don't look for the easy way out. They learn from previous mistakes and hold themselves accountable for their choices. Winners take equal responsibility for their successes and failures.

Villains, often times, take credit when things are going great. As soon as things take a turn, they bail. We call this villain Pity Party Pat. Pat wants people to feel sorry for them. Pat understands people who feel sorry for them are less likely to hold Pat accountable for their choices.

Someone operating with a villain at the helm can't be a winner. Winners don't find scapegoats. When a winner thinks about whining, they know the time has come to stop and evaluate. Because villains place blame elsewhere, they are unable to accept fault and therefore cannot resolve issues or overcome obstacles.

I want to introduce you to the term vicpion. A vicpion is a place where those who have not quite mastered the ability to operate in the mentality of a winner live. This is a midpoint, a place where you are not allowing your inner villain or hero to take the lead. Vicpion was built for heroes in hybrid with characteristics of both superhero and villain, think Batman Dark Knight. The vicpion is less whiny than the villain but still doesn't take full responsibility for their actions or consistently operate as a winner.

Someone who thinks they are a winner, or aspires to be a winner, can easily become stuck on vicpion. They've had small victories over big issues and are sitting back on their laurels becoming complacent. It is easy to do. Remember, complacency is your red light.

Becoming a winner happens in three distinct steps of equal importance: overcome your whining; act on your wishes; maintain your winning streak. Winning is work. It takes a while to train yourself to peak form. All the great superheroes had practice rounds and lots of failures before finding their groove. Shazam, as represented in the 2019 movie, is one of the most entertaining versions but David Parker and Clark Kent struggled too.

Do you remember the question I asked you at the beginning of this chapter? Now that you've had a moment to deep dive ask yourself these questions:

Do you covet their superhero's abilities or is there something inside of them that draws you in?

What qualities, not abilities, do you see translating into your daily life?

Can you see yourself as that kind of superhero?

If your answer is no, let's address what steps you need to reach a level in life that allows you to be the hero of your own story.

If you answered yes, you just might be ready to operate with a winning mentality.

The Whiner

The whiner makes very little moves, if any. Often, they are stuck at a red light in their life. They live in their mind, making excuses, building emotional walls and walking through life with a mask on. This is the level that a lot of individuals spend their time combatting. To win you must overcome this level. This is the very beginning stage of becoming a winner. At this stage nothing is happening except for the pampering and nurturing of Pity Party Pat. The whiner hides behind masks, only active long enough to build up walls. They have not discovered their internal capacity to win. They have yet to tap into their inner strengths and abilities. The whiner lives in a place of complacency, unmotivated to become more. The whiner is stunted, rooted in denial. The whiner is too busy with the internal dialogue to see their abilities and potential.

The Wisher

The wisher is at the midpoint of becoming a winner. Wishers operate as a winner but have not yet mastered the ability to maintain a winning mindset. The wisher remains self-conscious, bound by the judgments of others. They have not yet taken time to internalize all their abilities and desires.

Winners are not looking to be pampered. They don't want sympathy either. It wasn't until I began living as a winner that I embraced my inner strength. When I began to share my own personal stories, I would think to myself, *I really hope people are not feeling sorry for me*. I didn't want others feeling sorry for me because I didn't feel sorry for myself. More importantly, that wasn't the point of the share. I share as a way to connect through common experiences or to provide an example. Overcoming happened because I never gave up. Did I want to give up at times? Of course! I knew that, for me, giving up was not a valid option. This didn't happen overnight. It took years to accomplish. It is an accomplishment that, on bad days, I know was worthwhile and on good days I take pride in.

The journey to becoming a winner is not easy but every lesson I was able to learn because of it was worth it. As I began to move from being a whiner to becoming a winner, there was a time I believed that being strong made me strong. The reality was that me being able to be me, was what actually made me strong. This was during the time I lived on Vicpoin, keeping my guard up, suspicious of the world, not allowing people in. I felt like if I handled everything with a smile, pretended everything was okay, that was reflective of the winner in me. I was wrong. That is not what it means to be a winner.

The ability to be strong is not the definition of being a winner. I became a winner only after I allowed myself to be vulnerable. There is strength in the ability to relinquish control of every part of life. That is the definition of being strong. There are too many parts to becoming a winner to expect to achieve your status in a week's time. Becoming a winner takes time, practice and development. It can not be rushed.

Once you become a winner, you are no longer concerned with how others perceive you. You are only concerned with how you see yourself. You will begin to make decisions that are in your best interests. Because you now know who you are, it won't be difficult to face truths about yourself. You will begin to evaluate if the way you see yourself, is also how you present yourself. By this time, you will be in a position to want to see everyone around you win. The uncomfortable part about this phase is understanding that not everyone in your life is prepared to win. This is a challenge because when you start changing, growing and evolving you will need to let go of some of the people in your life. You will be different. People unable to respect or take an interest in your best self don't deserve the pleasure of your company. The winner is very much in tune to who they are, which helps them face this dilemma. Your emotional dependence on, and connection to, people will need to be evaluated. This is part of developing into a winner.

Winners don't throw their successes in the faces of others. They don't ignore them either. Figuring out how to work through this was very tough for me. Part of it was because I was not clear yet on who I was. This caused me to people please. I continued to play the role and downplay my abilities. This also fed into the part of me that was closed off, the part that kept everything to herself. I didn't trust what people would say or do with new information.

When I began my winning journey, I learned that I did not have to dim my light just to please others. I discovered that I needed to walk, live and always stand in, my truth no matter what. I was beginning to become liberated, freed from the mental bondage that plagued my mind. As long I was in that bondage, the champion mentality would never have been able to develop. Think about how many times you've stopped yourself from doing something you've wanted to do because of the way you felt others would armchair quarterback you? Winners have developed the ability to recognize their own feelings while considering the feelings of others. Having balance is very important. You can get caught up being overly obsessed with winning in much the same way you previously did with losing. This is not the outcome you want. Be sure not to get stuck in this trap.

Winning, and becoming a winner, should not hijack your logic. Winning, like a fine wine, is only perfected over time. You will not be perfect. If you are winning you don't want to be. There is no growth in perfection. Winning means you are working, every day, to be a better version of yourself.

When you are becoming a winner, it is not a race to finish or a contest for best. The only person you are claiming victory over is the old version of yourself. The great thing about that is you already know all your weaknesses! If you plan to stay a winner, you are going to have to remember the importance of patience. The art of practicing patience will be vital to the sustainability of your journey as a winner. You are not in a race to see who can finish first. There is no finish line. There is only maintenance. Maintaining equals balance and balance is perfect. When you are in maintenance you are living your perfect life. Staying a winner is an everyday goal.

Content, Comfort, Complacent

We have a normal. As you move outside of your comfort zone, what was once the unknown and frightening becomes your new normal. ~Robin Sharma, Motivational Speaker

I've built this information on the concept of a traffic light. Red is complacency - stagnation. Yellow is comfort – caution, don't slide into complacency. Green is content – because you are working your winning plan.

As a winner you will need to learn the pitfalls of becoming complacent. Complacency traps us. It usually keeps us stagnant. If we are in a state of complacency, we will not continue to strive or achieve more. Don't confuse complacency with comfort. Someone can be grateful for where they are in their lives and still work toward learning and growing as they continue to develop as a person.

Complacency is feeling secure and pleased while unaware of a potential danger or defect. Complacency stops progress. When we become complacent, we think we are in an okay position. Winners keep growing, keep evolving. They know in time there will always need to be adjustments because life is ever-changing.

I fell into the complacency trap and I was taught a very hard lesson because of it. I thought I'd arrived. I was an independent, accomplished, career-oriented, strong woman in her mid-30's. I had overcome life's obstacles and beaten the odds. I thought I was living the life. I was happy. It seemed as if, for once, my love life and career were truly in sync.

I became complacent. I stopped going after my dreams because I was doing great. I was making six figures doing what I wanted to do. I was driving what I wanted to drive. I was traveling where I wanted to travel. I thought I could ride this wave for the long haul. I set aside my personal plans because I loved what I was doing. That is right, you can be doing what you love, and actively do things that will also get you closer to achieving other aspirations. I spent so much time, energy and effort building the dreams of others, I failed to recognize the light of my own dream growing ever-dim.

Every now and again I would feel a nudge, become inspired, work on my dream a bit but, eventually, I would get "too busy". When the nudge came, it always seemed as though there was never enough time to work on the vision in my heart. The reality was it was easy to work hard for others. It allowed me to be lazy. I had become complacent, collecting my steady paycheck. It's crazy when I think of how hard I worked for others, too afraid to put that same energy into my own dream.

Winners don't allow anyone to prevent them from achieving their goals. When I was complacent, I was giving up on my dream. I didn't want to give up the dream but was willing to do it to avoid judgment. Winners don't give others that much power. The perceived judgment of others was my fear. My internal reaction to the fear was pessimism. Had I continued that way of thinking I would not be where I am today.

Ask yourself, what part of your life do you view through a pessimistic lens? Winners cannot win with a mindset riddled with negativity. If you want to win, and be a winner, you need to shut down the pessimistic narrative. It is not congruent with the mindset of a winner but rather a roadblock to it. If you find yourself with people who doubt your abilities you need to evaluate your circle.

You must understand the difference between being content verses being complacent. When someone is content, they are not anxious for anything or rushing the process. When you are content, you are grateful for where you are in your life, but you continue doing things to improve, challenge and better yourself. When you are complacent, you are stuck. You are not doing anything to improve yourself. Winners know how to be content without becoming complacent.

Be content and enjoy the journey of becoming a winner. Don't rush the process, you might bypass a concept needed to maintain the winning mindset. Develop yourself as a stable winner. Accept that not everyone around you will understand your progress. That's okay. Their understanding is irrelevant to your success.

As you move forward on your journey to becoming a winner, don't become complacent. Winners move differently than the average person. Keep that in mind when negative thoughts enter your mind.

Below are chapter summary questions for you to answer.

What superhero best describes you and why?

_____
_____
_____
_____

What are the things you need to do so that you don't get stuck on vicpion?

_____
_____
_____
_____

What do you need to do to ensure you are able to become your own hero?

_____
_____
_____
_____

What is your biggest takeaway from this chapter?

_____
_____
_____
_____

How will you apply that takeaway to your life this week?

_____
_____
_____
_____

Chapter 11

Setting goals and crushing them

"Focused, hard work is the real key to success. Keep your eyes on the goal, and just keep taking the next step towards completing it. If you aren't sure which way to do something, do it both ways and see which works better."

~John Carmack

The first step to crushing your goals is to set them. There are people who walk around every day without guidance, the ability to focus, or a plan for their life. They wake up with no direction and go to bed the same way. Without a road map, they wander aimlessly through life. I am in no way discouraging the free-spirits out there because I know plenty of free-spirited winners. I'm saying if you want to be successful and maintain your winning mindset then you are going to have to set some goals for yourself.

When you are preparing to achieve goals, you need to consider how the results of that goal will fit in with your life plan. We can set goals that keep us from making mistakes, or we can set goals that move us forward in life.

When I was pregnant and planning to attend grad school, I had my plan all laid out. It matched up with my life perfectly. Class orientation was the first week of December, my daughter was due mid-December and classes started in January. I had a clear goal, going back to school. I shared that with my mom and she was all for it. I shared it with my husband and he asked, 'Why are you doing that?' I was confused as to why he was asking me why I wanted to better myself. At the time I felt it was part of his way of trying to control me. Had I allowed his response to influence my decision, I wouldn't be where I am today. Don't allow anyone to have that much power over the goals you have set for your life.

Have you ever set a goal you felt was a bit out of reach? Have you ever given up on a goal because you became discouraged? If you answered yes to either question, then this is an important chapter in your journey.

Crushing your goals is the theme of this chapter. Thinking about it reminds me of the movie Godzilla, when the giant sea monster emerged stepping on buildings and crushing them.

To help me visualize myself crushing a goal I imagine Michael Jordan or Vince Carter dunking a basketball. Just the visualization, the energy it gives me, is motivation to keep crushing the goals I set for myself. Think about the image that comes to mind when you envision crushing a goal. Hold it in your mind for a few minutes. Every time you take a step toward crushing a goal and need a little motivation, recall that image as inspiration to push you forward.

These are all question you need to explore as you prepare to reach your goals:

What are the things you want for yourself?

_____
_____
_____
_____

What is it going to take to get you there?

_____
_____
_____
_____

What is it going to cost you? (emotionally, physically, mentally, etc.)

_____
_____
_____
_____

How will you muster up the courage to keep going in the face of an adverse response from your community?

_____
_____
_____
_____

It will be important for you to identify what type of goal you are setting. The different types of goals include life goals, personal goals, academic or career goals and family goals.

Personal Goals: Personal goals include things like improving your health, expanding your problem-solving skills, opening your lines of communication or becoming self-aware. You can delve further into categories including emotional, financial, interpersonal and physical goals. No matter the title, your personal goals are for you as an individual. Personal goals include hobbies, volunteer work and community outreach. They are quality of life goals that, in some way, add to your individual existence.

Career and Academic Goals: Academic-based goals may include seeking a higher education, furthering education courses, improving your grades, hiring a tutor, graduating, taking up a trade or vocational training.

Career goals can include educational goals such as professional seminars, extended learning, apprenticeships and internships. The category expands to include career paths such as military or diplomacy, titles you'd like to hold and ownership goals.

I can remember looking for a job. The goal I set for myself was to apply to at least 20 different job listings a day. It was not always fun, nor did I want to do it, but it was necessary in order for me to achieve my goal.

Eventually, the dedication and follow through paid off. I began to get interviews. I even received several offers. I set a goal, I stayed focused and I did what was necessary to achieve my daily goal.

Family Goals: Family goals are the goals we set for our families. They can include finding a life partner, starting a family or spending more time with relatives. Whatever the goal, it includes others.

Friends are family too. Not everyone has a mom, dad, sister or brother. Maybe your friends are closer to you than blood. You define your family. This category is for whomever fits.

Relationship Goals: Relationship goals expand beyond your life partner. You may have a goal of improving your communication skills, putting your trust in others or becoming more connected to the people around you. Relationship goals keep us from self-isolation. They remind us we are not alone in the world. The more we connect with others on a deep level, the more we begin to feel a sense of belonging.

There are other goal categories. These are just the most widely discussed. Goals can also overlap; family and relationship are great examples. Don't spend time on the label. Whatever the goal, make sure you see it through to the end. Determine what goals you have and develop a plan to incorporate them into your life in stages.

When setting your goals be sure to set reasonable timelines that are realistic. Don't overcommit or overextend yourself attempting to take on too much too soon. Despite being excited about your newly created goal, watch out for the resolution pitfall. This is the point when people have good intentions, but fail to commit or follow through. When setting your goal set reasonable timelines for completing the tasks associated with achieving the goal.

You can have multiple goals in different stages of completion. You may be completing your master's degree as one goal while planning to open a business and trying your hand at learning a new knitting technique to unwind. Maybe you're in the first semester of your degree journey, the beginning stages, but your business may be weeks away from opening. Regardless of where you are in a goal's plan, you should be reviewing and adjusting on a consistent basis.

The idea of adjusting is in almost every chapter of this book. Learning to be patient and flexible is essential to becoming a winner. The more you follow the steps in this guide, the more normalized each will become in your life. To achieve either you must be open to, and become comfortable with, change.

Winners create goals for every area of their lives. Their goals are roadmaps to navigate their desired outcome. A winner is clear about the goals they develop and they take the time required to build a plan of successful execution. They have built-in contingency efforts because they have thought through the process thoroughly. They don't give up on a goal because it is not turning out the way they expected. They adjust the goal accordingly.

Before you can execute your goal, you must evaluate its purpose in your life. When setting goals ask yourself:

What goal do I have?

_____
_____

_____
_____
_____

What is the purpose of this goal?

_____
_____
_____
_____

When do I consider the goal achieved?

_____
_____
_____
_____

What do I expect from the achievement?

_____
_____
_____
_____

Results Over Process

While you prepare to set goals, and are in the middle of achieving your goals, the G.O.A.L. model will help you maintain focus on the result.

G = Gather information about the intended purpose of the goal.

> You must take time to gather information about your intended goal. This may mean researching steps you need to take to accomplish your goal, such as certifications, possible time frames for completion and researching alternatives ways to meet the same end. Everything you need to better prepare yourself to build your plan should be clear at the end of this process. This is where your plan of action is established.

O = Observe potential obstacles and prepare to J.U.M.P. over them.

When looking at the intended goal, and plan of action, begin to identify hurdles and obstacles that will detour you, or make achieving your goal more difficult. Plan for the unexpected. Expect hurdles and know how you'll J.U.M.P. them. You can't plan for every obstacle or hurdle, but you can prepare for every foreseeable one. This will allow your plan to stay on track and keep your energy up. It is part of the planning process for achieving your goal. At the end of this phase your plan for achieving your goal is complete.

A = Accept the results of your plan.

No matter what the ending result, embrace the journey and its lessons as you move forward. If you need to tweak your approach and start over, do that. If the plan does not deliver the goal don't get discouraged. Learn from the experience and give it another shot. Be proud of your efforts and take time to internalize the lessons. Develop a new plan if the goal remains.

L = Learn from the experience and start over again.

Even if you somehow missed the mark on our goal, know that the execution of the goal was not in vain. You set a goal, made a plan and carried it out. That is more than many will do in a lifetime. That's what makes you a person with a winning mindset!

If you succeeded, track how that success aligns with your expectations. Make sure there is no further work needed to call it a successfully executed plan.

You put your all into it and for that you should be grateful to, and proud of, yourself. Not many people can set goals, let alone make them happen. You were ahead of the curve at, operating in the winning, not a whiner, mindset. Set the goal, crush the goal, rinse and repeat….

Dealing with life can cause our worlds to become so busy we loose focus. We have bills to pay, work that needs to be done, the kids need to be raised, pets need to go for a walk, etc. Don't get swept up in the rhythm of life. That's complacency. Having goals provides perspective to life. Consistent self-evaluation forces us to check the bulbs in our stoplight to make sure the light remains fully functioning. Focus is hard to maintain. That's why plans are required. They allow us to step toward our goals in manageable increments.

Winners are not perfect. Nobody is perfect. Winners improve how they respond to life events through practiced planning, and/or preparation. The more you consider goals and outcomes, the better equipped you can become at mentally engaging foresight. When we take the time to think about possible outcomes it changes the way we look at the situations that are presented. We are better able to break unhealthy behavioral cycles and recognize patterns that may emerge.

Moving On

I remember when I was preparing for grad school and I knew I hated math. I worked with a lady who was already enrolled in the program. I discovered she was no longer in the program and asked her why. She said it was just too hard, that she could not pass statistics after taking it twice and being on academic probation. I was so afraid of meeting the same fate that I thought of withdrawing my application from the program. Thankfully I recognized that she had made the choice to quit. I had a choice to not decide my future based solely on someone else's experience. I am thankful that I did not allow her decision to dictate the choice I made for my life. I almost aborted my plan because I internalized someone else's fears and experiences, making them my own.

Winners win every day. They show up when they don't feel like it. They set goals that force them to put the work in. They believe in themselves even when others don't. They have the capacity to do all this because they have taken the time to get to know themselves.

Winners don't always set easy goals. Some goals will be easier than others, but overall, the winner sets challenging goals that push them pass their comfort zones. It is in the uncomfortable areas of life that we grow.

Winners are open, and willing, to putting the work in to get them to where they need to be. They know there is no easy way out. They take accountability for the goals they've set and do what it takes to be successful, including altering plans and changing goals.

Winners Don't Whine

Now that you have set the goal, don't get discouraged because of the amount of work and effort it will take to be achieved. Winners don't whine or get weak when it comes to doing the necessary work. Even when the road to achievement gets rough, winners don't whine. Winners don't quit and they don't waver in their winning abilities. Winners don't sit on the sidelines or give up. They use the G.O.A.L. model to assist them on their way.

The Mindful Winner

There will be goals you develop for your life that are meant only for you. This can be a challenge when you become excited about the progress you see and its impact on the quality of your life. Be mindful of the things you share with others. Protect your goals. Once you achieve a goal feel free to shout it from the rooftops. Recognize the difference between being a secret keeper and protecting your future.

When I first decided to write my book I was overly excited and told anyone who wanted to listen. It wasn't boastful, I was just happy and ready to have it become my reality. I had set my goal and I was doing the work. When my manuscript was lost I was sad and frustrated, but I was mostly embarrassed. I had shared my dream with all these people, and nothing had come of it. I worried people would question my authenticity.

It was my own mental hang up that derailed me, not the corruption of the thumb drive. I could have started over from my notes, but I didn't. I learned from that experience. My plan didn't include contingencies and that lesson had to be learned. The reality was I was not yet operating with a winning mindset so completion was impossible, even if the thumb drive had not become corrupted. There is no guarantee some other obstacle would not have tripped me up. Despite getting sidetracked, taking the long way to get here, I was ultimately able to complete my goal, but not until it was appropriate for me to do so.

When you are developing your goal, the goal can be fragile. You must handle the development and creation of your goal with care. Protect it as you would an unborn child. Imagine your goal as a baby in the womb. Nobody can see it. They see the growth of the belly and the changes in mom, but they don't see the baby. It is not until the baby has been born that the full potential of the child is first able to be evaluated. This is precisely what I am suggesting for your goals. Don't share them before they are ready to be evaluated.

You can share that you are working toward goals. If you feel the need to share every detail, ask yourself, why? What are you getting from sharing everything about the goals you have set for yourself? Oftentimes people share early to give the same rush they believe achieving the goal accomplishes, they think that speaking is equal to actualizing. It is a brain chemistry reaction not unlike confusing lust for love. In both instances, only the latter is sustainable.

Sharing parts of your plan can help keep you accountable to the goal at hand. This will serve as a means to keep you focused on achieving your goal. Think of it in terms of sharing steps of your goal but not the goal itself.

Whose Goal Is It?

When a winner sets a goal for themselves, they don't get caught up in whether people will agree with them. They understand that they are not living to please others. They live to better themselves. It is okay to move in silence. There is nothing wrong with protecting your goals as you develop them.

If you are in a committed relationship, I encourage you to have a conversation with your mate, out of respect, if your goal will disrupt the relationship emotionally, financially or spiritually. Do not give up on your goal just because they don't want you to do it. Not everyone wants you to progress past where you are currently. If you have identified a goal that will help to improve your life, make you better in some way, then who cares what they think. Make it happen. Elevate the relationship once the paradigm has shifted. You are too powerful, purposed, strong and beautiful to allow others to stunt your growth.

As we set goals and crush them, it is wise that we ask for guidance. Be wise about the goals you are setting for yourself. You don't want to set unobtainable or unrealistic goals. If you have a weight goal for example, timeline and effort must be accounted for along with your body type. This will serve to ensure you are not setting a goal of losing 200 pounds in a month. Even with weight loss surgery that goal is not a realistic one. When setting a goal look past the obvious and look at how you plan on maintaining the end result once it is achieved.

When I was thinking about setting up a non-profit cancer foundation, I spoke with an advisor and I found out that, just because I created and founded the organization, did not mean I would always be the decision maker for the foundation. I would have a board to answer to. I explained to her that I wanted to always be in control of the decisions and direction of the board. She said to me, 'Cortina, what do you ultimately want to see happen as a result of creating this foundation?' Finding out I would not always directly control the final decisions caused me to think about the direction of the goal I had set. It made me think long and hard about my motivation for creating a foundation. I had to think about altering my plans and personal goals for the organization's development. What was the reason I needed to be in charge of the decision-making if I was ultimately the one creating the mission and the vision? Was it my lack of trust and inability to let go that prevented me from starting the foundation? I suspect it was a knee-jerk reaction to having had my previous creative plan taken by the care facility that dismissed me following the acquisition. It could have also been because I wasn't at a place in my life yet where I was comfortable having others carry out my dreams.

Why or what motivates us to create the goals we do?

Why have you selected this goal?

Don't get in the habit of selecting goals because you are chasing gold or an ideal. Be patient with the process. Be mindful of the goals you set and the reason why you feel like quitting before the goal is achieved. Some people easily create great goals that are obtainable. However, they fail to plan or never see them through. Remember that winners see goals through to the end. They are able to see them through to the end because they spend time planning the process for the goal to be executed and achieved. There will be times when a goal will no longer serve a purpose in the winner's life, or it has to be adjusted to fit a changed need of the winner. Winners understand that, in order to win, goals must be a part of the winning mindset. Ask God to grant you wisdom and understanding when creating goals. Seek His guidance and strength for patience to direct your path.

Accountability Revisited

Hold yourself accountable and take responsibility for the things that worked, and equally, for the things that didn't work. If you set a goal that didn't work, go back and figure out what mistakes were made and what could have been done differently.

I can reflect on my own life and identify the many times I was able to set a goal and crush it in the process. Were some of those times scary? Absolutely, but I kept going, never giving up, especially when I wanted to. When I was preparing to take the exam to become a licensed mental health counselor my goal was to study intensively for the six days leading up to test day. I had everything mapped out. I told myself, *'If I don't pass, I'll just schedule to take it again,'* because if I had put too much pressure on myself the stress would have been more harmful than good. I took the test. When I found out I passed, I was ecstatic. I had prayed about it. I had prepared myself. I believed in myself. Passing was my winning result.

The time I beat cancer was another example of setting a goal. I told myself that my goal was not to give up but to get up and fight every day. I believe that our thoughts have power, and our faith and belief in our abilities are what help to keep us focused and on the right path. Not everything is going to go the way you plan it to. I didn't know if I would be living today or if there were other plans for my destiny. One thing I did know was I was not going to give up, and that my goal was to fight. It was hard but I put in my mind that there are others out there who were going through harder situations. With every battle I faced, there was a goal created to help me push through.

Impossible or Possible?

I never would have thought some of the things I made it through or accomplished were possible. I have learned there are times when people can believe in your goals more than you. Sometimes people are able to see your potential and greatness before you do. I think I've always known that I could accomplish anything I set my mind to do, however there were times when I questioned my ability to do so. During these times there were people that would encourage me to keep going. While I doubted about my abilities their belief in me never wavered.

It is so important for you to believe in your own abilities. When it came to success I was never given a playbook. I had to learn as I went along. I learned a lot of tough, hard lessons. Despite the lack of handholding, I refused to give up or fail. Winners realize that just because things don't go their way or the end is not what they had hoped, that does not mean it was a fail. A fail is when you give up. A fail is when you don't try. A fail is when you stop believing in yourself. A fail is when you undermine your abilities. You were built for this, lean on your internal strength to carry you through.

When setting goals, believe in your talents, have faith that everything will work out. These are the mental keys to success. You can't give your goal 100% if you don't believe in yourself and are doubting your abilities.

You must have vision for your life so that the real winner inside of you can emerge. If you don't create roadmaps for your life, how will you know where you're headed? When setting goals, don't forget to plan for potential barriers. What are the things that may detour you? Build flexibility into your goals. Inflexible targets make adjusting to obstacles more difficult.

Whatever It Takes

If you want to crush your goals, discipline will need to be a skill you develop. This comes along with taking responsibility for your actions. Be disciplined enough to do the things you need to do without making excuses.

All of these are part of focusing in on your goal. No matter what you want to have happen in your life, you will have to ask yourself if you really believe that it can happen. We often say we want things but don't really believe that the goal is worth obtaining, we are worthy or that it can happen. It sounds good when we share our dreams but we really don't envision that what we want will happen. Those are not dreams. They are fantasies. Working the G.O.A.L. model will help you recognize the difference.

Value yourself enough to dismiss anything that disrupts your life, your mindset, your value, your worth or the goals you have. Don't listen to the pessimistic messages that enter your mind. Don't allow situations to distract you from the things you have set your mind to do.

Set the goal and win, is the chant I want you say to yourself every day. Say it with me… Set the goal and win, set the goal and win, set the goal and win! Stand in the mirror in the morning and speak into your life. Tell yourself I am a winner, I will win. Start your day with positive steps. Begin to see the difference it will make.

One of the first positive steps that can be implemented into your daily routine are positive affirmations. They help jumpstart your day, allowing you to begin on a positive note. This gets you in the habit of speaking positivity into your life and inviting positive energy to flow.

Don't doubt the progress you've made. Be willing to take risks. Chase down your dreams until they become your reality. Don't be afraid to fall. Falling, some call it failing, is a part of every winner's story.

Having a G.O.A.L. keeps doubts from overtaking your mind because all doubts should have a contingency plan. When you get used to listing out the reasons why it won't work, reference your plan to get back on track.

Remember The Why

What is your why? Why do you want to be a winner and what is pushing you to win? Everyone thinks that being a winner, a champion, means that it's always a party or that everything is always good. Part of that is true but there is another side to winning that people don't talk about. That is the lonely side of winning. As mentioned earlier, not everyone is going to be able to go with you as you travel down your journey to becoming a winner. Winners often make sacrifices and tough decisions. Winners risk having to miss out on parties, sleeping in, living anyway they want to, hanging out with friends, going to bed early, not having responsibilities, they risk being judged, and they risk having people not believe in them.

Don't get in the habit of saying an affirmation because it sounds good. Believe in your ability to win and W.O.W. Every day you must remember your why. Remember why you can W.O.W. Even when no one is in your ear cheering you on, supporting you, or there with you, and know that you can, and will, win. If you begin to feel discouraged as you navigate your journey to becoming and discovering the winner within, remember why you can and will succeed if you continue to believe in your abilities.

You are now ready to make a plan and crush your goal.

Below are chapter summary questions for you to answer.

List three (3) goals for your life.

_____
_____
_____

Identify the steps needed to ensure the goal is accomplished.

_____
_____
_____

Identify potential barriers to completing each goal.

_____
_____
_____

How will you overcome each barrier?

_____
_____
_____

List 5 reasons why you can achieve the goals you have set.

_____
_____
_____

How will you know when you've crushed your goal?

_____
_____
_____

How will the goal you set today help you tomorrow?

_____
_____
_____
_____

What is one (1) step you will take today towards a goal listed above?

_____
_____
_____
_____

Chapter 12

The Winner Evolution

"Look around you. Everything changes. Everything on this earth is in a continuous state of evolving, refining, improving, adapting, enhancing and changing. You were not put on this earth to remain stagnant."

~Dr. Steve Maraboli, Life, the Truth, and Being Free

For just a moment, stop and think about who you are and the reason why you were created. This may cause you to take pause and consider your answer. As I began working through this part of the winning process, on finding my purpose, I had to put on my big girl panties and do the work. I could no longer hide behind the walls I'd designed into the architecture of the life I'd built for myself. That was a life I no longer needed. Masks had to be thrown away and walls needed to be demolished. I was starting to hold myself accountable, confronting things within that I didn't think I was ready for. I remember someone asking me if I cried. I brushed off the inquiry replying, 'Yes, I cry.' I really didn't think anything more about it. It wasn't until later, that I was going through a situation, when I remember asking myself, *'Who are you and when did you stop crying?'* I would always say I was sensitive, because I cried during movies or cute Instagram videos. When I began to really look at it, I discovered that I didn't cry, or allow myself to feel, what it was that I may have been going through. I would experience whatever it was and put my true emotions on the shelf to collect dust. I did not take the time to deal with how I felt about things. I became disconnected from my reality. I didn't take time out for self-care and my emotional needs suffered.

A true winner understands the importance of self-care and that, ensuring their own emotional wellness takes precedent over everything and everyone else. Though I had removed the masks and torn down the walls, I was still holding onto those shelved emotions, trying to move them into my new life without first seeing if it made sense to keep. It was time to clean up and pack for my new life.

Whatever negative emotions you are facing in life, remember they are fleeting. This means never make a permanent decision relying on temporary emotions. Think of your feelings as house guests. House guests never stay forever. They come to visit and then they leave. This is the same with our emotions. One minute you may be angry, however two hours later, you might be in a better headspace. Your emotions might be preventing you from resolving hurts from your past or stopping you from being able to forgive others or yourself. You might even be afraid to revisit tough periods from your past out of fear of the emotions that you will feel. However, it might become crucial to revisit certain periods in your life to ensure you have thoroughly processed whatever needed to be worked through. This needs to happen. It is necessary so that you can be clear about where you're headed. Hopefully, things that have challenged you have been fully resolved or are on track to being resolved.

We discussed the importance of getting to know who you are and adjust to the circumstances you may be facing. Now it's time to go a little deeper into the evolution of knowing yourself and discovering your purpose.

As I continued down the winner's journey another lesson that was difficult for me to internalize was putting myself first. I was so used to making concessions and making sure everyone else was okay, that I was lost in the process. My own emotional sanity was on the line. This new insight required that I was willing to leave people, places and things behind. Sometimes we get so attached to people and things, we are unable to realize how detrimental they are to our purpose. Take a long, hard look at the things you allow into your life. This is another part of embracing your journey.

When I had cancer, my hair fell out. I was fine with that. I expected it to happen. It really wasn't devastating to me when it finally did. As I went through my journey, I would share it openly with others and what I looked like on the outside did not bother me. I was secure in my skin, so thankful to be alive that nothing else mattered to me. When I was diagnosed with lupus in 2013, it was pretty debilitating and painful. I didn't really begin to experience cosmetic effects until a few years later. One midsummer day in 2018, I started styling my hair and saw a large section was missing. I began to look through my scalp and I realized I had several large bald spots. I was devastated. I couldn't understand why the loss of hair was affecting me the way it was. I had lost my hair before, so why was it such a big deal now?

I came to realize that it was the way I viewed my hair loss. I expected to lose my hair during my cancer battle, so I had mentally planned for the obstacle. Losing my hair to lupus was unexpected. It caused me to question how I viewed myself. Dealing with the increased activity of my lupus became particularly challenging. I had begun dating again after another unhealthy five-year relationship ended. Part of me wanted to consider other people's feelings about my daily life. Lupus was a part of me now. Although I wanted to be able to say, 'They either accept it or they don't,' I still was resistant to show that part of myself to others. I didn't want to be rejected because of it but transparency is hard when it means your dream can become further out of reach or taken out of your control. I've never wanted anyone to feel sorry for me. I also didn't want to keep this from individuals who needed the information to make an informed decision about their own life path. It took me a long time to be okay with showing someone the physical scars left by lupus. When I did decide to get into a serious relationship, I reminded myself that I wanted to be vulnerable and transparent. I wanted to give parts of me that I had never shared with anyone else, I wanted to do something different. I wanted to learn to let my guard down and have a genuine connection.

While casually dating I rarely showed weakness or vulnerability. I wouldn't allow myself to get close to anyone emotionally. I began to question if I would ever allow someone to see the real me or get close enough to see into my soul. I was afraid that, by allowing people to get close they would see the things I kept buried. I had to trust my intuition. When it was time to give myself permission to be vulnerable and open up to the person who was deserving, I did.

As you develop the winner in you, you will have to evaluate your views of people and the world. How does the way you see yourself impact your connections with others? Winners understand that fear of their real selves may serve as fuel to self-sabotaging behaviors. I had to realize that it wasn't the guys I was dating who were the problem, it was me. My inability to be vulnerable, to trust others with my truth, that was on me to handle. I had selective vulnerability. I was okay sharing the things about me that made me look strong and I would minimize exposure to things that could cause my strength to be questioned. I had to learn that if people could not, or would not, accept my truth then they didn't deserve me.

I had taken off the masks, but I had not yet demolished the walls. I had become hard, jaded and, to some extent, cold. I had decided I would not allow anyone to take advantage of me, ever again. No one knew the real me. No one knew my heart. No one understood me. I made sure of it. I built impenetrable walls around me. I was fine cutting people out of my life. My sole purpose was the protection of my heart. I wouldn't give anyone all of me though I made them believe I had. I finally had to ask myself, *who am I when no one is around?*

I realized that I wanted the softer side of me back. I wanted to be able to connect with the sensitivity my heart was built to handle. I had been denying its growth out of fear of being taken advantage of. I needed to understand that being emotional did not make me weak, it made me human. My ability to be in touch with my emotions, identifying how I felt about a situation and understanding how it may or may not have affected me needed nurturing. Not being able to feel, live, stand and be in my truth needed to change. This wasn't the life of a winner. If I was going to be a true winner, I needed to be a winner in all areas of my life. I could not speak to people every day about improving their lives if I wasn't doing what I needed to do to improve mine. I was done faking it. I was done pretending. I was done living in emotional bondage, a slave to my past.

In order to elevate and go higher, you will need to leave some of the places that are comfortable. You will have to get past the pain and work through the shallow shadows. Shallow shadows are things that we know are issues, but we only deal with the surface portion of the issue. Dealing with shallow shadows, can sometimes make you think that you are dealing with the core of the issue, but it is a trick. You are only doing enough work to feel good in the moment.

If you want to win, your ability to connect to other winners will need to become a skill you develop. Surrounding yourself with others who want to win is important because of the connectedness and accountability it brings. It is easy to get caught up in negativity. The less you allow it to enter your life, the better you'll be. If you've gone through some things, sharing with others will decrease the lasting negative effects. Your experience may also be what they need to help them be motivated. They may find you inspiring and BOOM, you've planted a seed in the life of a future winner.

Never underestimate the power of your words. It's not uncommon for people to keep things to themselves. There are some people who don't want to help, don't want anyone but them to succeed. Don't be one of those people. It is possible for everyone to win. You lose nothing by providing help, guidance or encouragement to others. A real winner understands that nothing will be taken away from them as a result of helping others. When you help others you indirectly help yourself. You never know when the favor will need to be returned.

Winners take a deep dive into their issues and resolve them. This diminishes the likelihood of them reappearing. We can sometimes ignore our issues too. I talked about burying mine in work goals. My life was all work and no play. It made me feel good, but my life was not balanced. Winners know that balance is key. What are you doing to keep your life in balance?

New Beginnings and Finding Peace

Wiping the slate clean is the area where you have cleared out all of the clutter, unresolved past hurt and disappointment in your life. You are able to see the path of your journey clearly. Now that you have reviewed each area of your life, and adjusted where needed, you can begin to discover, or rediscover, your purpose.

Your purpose may be revealed in the goals that you set for yourself or in the connections you make and lives you touch. Be clear who the winner should be. Trusting the process encompasses the notion that winners are patient with the process.

Achieving your goal may be the portal to helping others discover their own purpose. When you act on your ambitions people are attracted to you. You may inspire them without their ever understanding why. Stop giving precious energy to people and causes that do not define, refine or reveal your purpose. Follow through with your goals and dreams no matter what. Work on taking time to discover your passions and purpose in life. Seek to find a deeper understanding of your truth and, once you find it, work to keep it at the forefront of your mind. This all comes as we continue to evolve as winners.

Evolution is a continuous process that is aligned with maintaining the winner in you. There will always be something in your life that needs adjustment. Once you are able to get to a place in your life where you are healing yourself, a sense of calm and peace will come over you if you allow it.

A Place for Peace

I was in search of peace but, the way I was filtering my world, there was no room for peace to enter. When learning to calm yourself and give peace permission to enter into your life, you will need to do a few things. You will need to envision what peace will look like in your life. What is peace to you and where does it fit?

A way you let peace into your life is to practice and incorporate guided imagery every day. Here is a quick guided imagery exercise for you.

Close your eyes. Breathe in deeply through your nose, and slowly release it through your mouth. As you are breathing, begin to see yourself inhaling peace, love, light, and healing. As you exhale release fear, doubt, shame, guilt and pain. Do this about 10 times, or until you began to feel your mood shifting. Continue to practice this exercise until it becomes an automatic process.

I was a person in positions of power for so long, but I had no idea who I was, let alone what peace would or could look like in my life. I had to find what peace meant to me and work on ways of granting permission for peace to enter into my life. I can say with certainty that I did the work, and I know that I have found my peace. I am fulfilling my purpose in life.

Writing this guide is part of my purpose. Helping you to find your purpose is part of my purpose. Inspiring you to win is part of my purpose. I always said I loved what I do for a living, and I would do it for free. That was, and is, true. Now I am in a place where not only am I able to live out my purpose, but I also have peace in my heart as I fulfill it. Get to a place where you can be at peace with fulfilling your purpose. I decided that if something risked my peace it wasn't worth it. You can begin to do this by evaluating situations that jeopardize your peace and ask yourself, 'Is my peace of mind really worth it?'

Take time to breathe, relax and slow down. Life isn't a race. Your purpose isn't going anywhere. It will still be there when you arrive. If you rush you risk your peace, and your peace of mind. Learn to believe in yourself so that you can show up and win every day, even when you don't feel like it.

Pace yourself. Know that, as long as you have set the groundwork, identified the goal and are focused on your purpose, there is nothing more you can do.

As you walk in your wining lifestyle, identify what peace looks like for you. Where is your peace? What are the things that you can do to get more of it? Resolve whatever it is in your life that is vexing you. Remind yourself that peace is a part of the process. Incorporate the Q.U.I.E.T. model into your life. The Q.U.I.E.T. model allows you to quiet your mind so that peace can enter.

(Q) = Quit Getting Distracted

> I know I told you winners never quit. This is the exception. If you are having a hard time focusing, it is likely due to a distraction. Distractions can be a problem for anyone aspiring to live the winning life. Distractions take away focus from your goals affecting your ability to concentrate on the things that need your attention. Whether it is an intentional or unintentional distraction, be mindful that distractions can, and will, serve as roadblocks.
>
> It is possible to self-sabotage your progress and ruin your ability to move forward. This happens subconsciously so that we don't have to do what's necessary to grow. This is usually because we are afraid to give our thoughts the time to grow into solutions for outstanding problems.

(U) = Utilize Your Resources

> Whatever you need, find a way to obtain it. Everything you need to better yourself is available. Identify the resources and use them to your advantage. Don't make excuses for not moving forward or obtaining the necessary resources. Sometimes we may question our ability to gather resources due to lack of information. Don't be afraid to ask for

assistance. There are people out there who have access to valuable resources. Ask for the help. Look for other alternatives to accessing and utilizing resources. Utilizing resources means just that, the ability to use what is at your disposal to help you get closer to your goal.

(I) = Invite Tranquility Into Your Life

This is something you will have to intentionally pursue. Give yourself permission to replace negative thoughts with positive ones. Light and dark do not coexist in nature. Your body is part of nature, so it is vital to actively invite peace and light into your life. Practice mindfulness techniques. Learn to center yourself. Incorporate thought-stopping techniques, replacing negative distressing thoughts with thoughts that are more positive and reaffirming.

(E) = Envision Yourself in a Place of Peace

You must begin to see yourself in a place of peace and calm. Chaos and confusion do not have to be a part of your life. Approach distress from a place of peace and embrace what comes as an opportunity to grow. If you are accustomed to craziness in your life, peace may never be able to enter your mind. Make room for peace and achieve peace of mind. You make room by setting boundaries and identifying the things that will create a place for peace to enter. A few examples include mindfulness, a calm safe place, guided meditation and deep breathing meditation exercises. Any of these will allow you to center, clearing your mind so that you have the mental and emotional space to create your place of peace.

(T) = Take a Time Out

As a winner, you should learn the importance of recharging your energy reserves. Don't allow people in your life to continuously take from you. Give yourself time so that you can be reenergized. It is okay to be still. You will have a better chance of focusing if your give yourself the time and space needed. Take a time out. This had always been an issue for me. Always on the run, I never gave myself the time to recharge. Everyone needs to reset and rejuvenate. This helps with the growth and development of the winner in you.

Now that you've learned how to add peace into your life, you will be held accountable and responsible for your own progress. Don't allow anyone to stunt your growth as a winner. Speak up for yourself and protect your peace. Don't allow others to dump in the space you have cleared for your peace to reside. Know when to block out the negative things that people try to bring into your life. You will be so busy winning, that you won't have time for other people's drama. Understand your limits and know that you are not obligated to give up your peace to appease others.

Don't allow people to dictate how you get to feel and when you get to feel it. You can have peace in every area of your life, just as you can win in every area of your life. Things might be hectic but that doesn't mean your peace has to suffer. When things get a little crazy, the peace you possess will help keep you calm through the storm. There is no need to get flustered. That only serves to conflate the situation. Be the calm. Control how you respond to the situation.

The Power is Yours

Keep reminding yourself that you have the power to win. Everything you need to be a winner with peace, you have at your fingertips. Use these resources and make a commitment to yourself. Identify your purpose and what it will take to fulfill your destiny. Walk with authority and believe that you can have what you want. Connect with other like-minded winners and make winning a part of your everyday life. It will not always be easy, but it will be worth it.

Enjoy the journey of learning everything you need to know about yourself. No one should know more about who you are than you do. Always take the time to evaluate and adjust. You will continue winning and, in the process, discover your purpose. You will find your why. Why you fought so hard to discover the winner within. Why you had to take the masks off in order to win. Why you tore down walls. Why you keep going through each day. Why you show up and operate in your hero mindset. Why you did the work to become a winner. You will stop asking why you, and start asking why not me. You are destined to be a successful winner.

Below are chapter summary questions for you to answer.

Identify what you think your purpose might be.

_____
_____
_____
_____

What steps are needed in order for you to fulfill that purpose?

_____
_____
_____
_____

What additional steps can you take to evolve into, and stay a winner?

_____
_____
_____
_____

What things can you do to protect your energy reserves?

_____
_____
_____
_____

Chapter 13

The Power to Seek Out, Access and Ask for Help

No one who achieves success does so without acknowledging the help of others.

The wise and confident acknowledge this help with gratitude.

~Alfred North Whitehead, philosopher

You're almost to the end of your development as a winner. One of the last things you need to do is make sure you have a strong support network to lean on when needed. Some people find it very difficult to reach out and ask for help. When this is the case ask yourself, 'Why is it difficult for me to ask for help?' Generally, the answer is an outstanding issue left to address. Shame, embarrassment, fear and pride all get in the way. Whatever it is, you need to identify and fix it. If you don't, you cannot win.

Once you've discovered who you are, it will be easier for you to ask for help. There are many ways in which people can ask for, and receive, the support they need. For the sake of the W.O.W. E.F.F.E.C.T. we'll refer to a specific model to guide you through the process and help you get the assistance you need.

Counsel

Counsel are individuals that help hold you accountable. These are the people who will be there to lift you up and encourage you when needed. The balanced counsel should consist of spiritual, secular and social counselors. These are the ones who will help to hold you up when you feel like you want to fall.

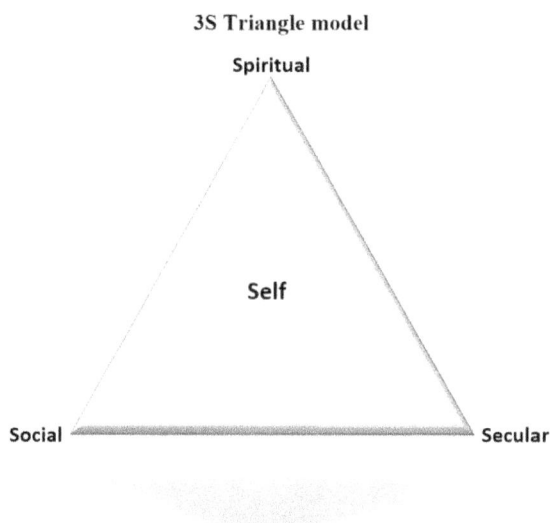

Let's take a closer look at the 3S model.

Spiritual Counsel

Spiritual counselors are individuals who speak to your spiritual side. They give you advice that keeps you in spiritual alignment. These individuals could be any of the following: pastor, spiritual leader, priest, prayer warrior, nun, elder, minister, prayer partner, or anyone with whom you connect spiritually. They will speak from a place of wisdom and will pray with you, and for you. This will be a person you trust to help you become, and remain spiritually strong.

Your spiritual counsel will use spiritual teachings and lessons to help you maintain the winner within. As with all your various counsel groups it will be vital that you are honest with them. It is also okay to have back up counsel. There may be times when you call on someone you know that can also feed your spirit. Reach out to them if your permanent spiritual counsel is unavailable.

Identify at least two (2) individuals that would fit into your spiritual counsel category?

1. _____

2. _____

If you are not able to come up with any, I would suggest you take time out to identify the characteristics that you would like a spiritual counselor to have. Once you have done this, you can then begin to search for someone who fits your needs. The only way to keep the 3S triangle balanced is to have the triangle complete.

Secular Counsel

Secular counselors are individuals that are paid, and entrusted, to hold you accountable. This will happen when you are doing things contrary to what you have planned, or that go against progressing toward your goal. Individuals in this category are not your everyday friends. They are specific individuals with very specific roles. The boundaries are a bit more ridged when it comes to interactions and exchanges. Individuals in the secular category include mentors, life coaches and therapists.

Mentor

Mentors serve as models. They show us how we can get to a place in our life where we know they have the skills to guide us toward. For the most part they have been where we are and are now where we want to go.

Mentors are essentially role models. They help give us guidance and show us what worked for them.

Therapist

Everyone can benefit from seeking out the expertise of a therapist. As a therapist, I think it is vital to have a therapist that you see regularly. Therapists are not only for those with problems, they are an essential part of your maintenance plan. Think about it like going to the gym. Initially you might go to get in shape. Once you've achieved the goal, you must maintain it by continuing to work out. Everyone needs that one person in their life who is neutral. This is where the therapist comes in to assist.

When you begin the journey of healing yourself, discovery of self is number one. This is not always easy. It is a very necessary part of the process. You must be willing to bare it all, at all costs. Of course, it won't feel good because change is often uncomfortable.

Not every therapist will be the right fit for you. I like to think of therapists as shoes. Sometimes it might be beneficial to try on a few until you find the one that fits you. Don't give up if you don't connect with the first therapist you come across, simply try another.

The therapist is there to help facilitate the process and bring your life to a deeper level of awareness. I remember when I was searching for a therapist, it took me months to find the right one. Being in the field, I was so afraid that my shortcomings might be shared. Despite the notion of confidentiality, and professional ethics rules, I still was hesitant to share my true feelings. That was fear winning plain and simple. In my mind, I was about to give someone the power to use all my perceived shortcomings against me. When I was finally able to find someone I began to share with her the things I had discovered about myself. It really was hard at times not to keep things inside. I had to remind myself of the things I would tell my own patients.

I would tell my patients that I can only process and explore the things you share with me. Your life is 100% of who you are. If we are in therapy and you only give me 75% of you, then I will only be able to process that 75%. That 25% that you refuse to share might be the part that keeps you in emotional bondage.

It is possible to be unaware that you are holding onto things. With the help of the right therapist, the things you might be holding onto may be revealed and resolved. I struggled to be honest with my therapist out of fear of judgment. I had to remind myself that the process was for me and, if I wanted to go further in my journey, fear could not be a part of it. One of the worse things you can do is lie to your therapist. What purpose would it serve? If you can't be honest with your therapist then don't waste the money.

Once you begin to heal yourself, some of the people around you will start to look different. You will have a heightened level of self-awareness and the life you once had. Once you bare it all, you will feel a weight has been lifted. You will still go through things but you will be better prepared, emotionally and mentally, to handle them. Therapy is a shedding process. View it as an onion or cabbage. You must peel back one layer to get to the next. The core, your core, is the destination.

Life Coach

The final person in this category is a life coach. Life coaches help cheer you on. They are your personal hype man. They will root for you and motivate you. They aren't therapists so they generally don't process and explore deep-seated issues. They help you to see yourself as more- they guide you to your greatness. The boundaries of a life coach are more relaxed than those of a therapist or mentor. Nonetheless, they can be very beneficial to your growth and development as a winner. They cheer for you but they are not your friend. They'll hold you accountable for meeting marks and help you talk through the goal and plan revisions.

The secular counsel group will help to push you past your comfort levels. They won't coddle you. They help you find your path to a greater self. They help to open the doors of self-actualization and allow you to obtain a deeper sense of self-awareness.

Identify at least three (3) individuals that would fit into secular counsel category in your life?

1. _____
   (The Mentor)

2. _____
   (The Therapist)

3. _____
   (The Coach)

Social Counsel

This category is composed of close friends, confidants, business partners, family members and/or romantic partners. This group is there for you. They are more than likely the ones you call when you need a shoulder to cry on or a sounding board. Everyone in your family or friends circle will not fit into this group, these are your starting lineup. Just because you consider someone to be family, doesn't mean they have your best interests at heart. Your social counselors are the ones you call when you want to hang out or have a good time. They will also be the ones to help lift your spirits.

The social counsel group can be viewed as the least proper group. The ones you wear your emotional sweats around. They are, in a sense, the lighter side of the triangle. They have seen you at your worst and they are the ones you want to celebrate with when you are at your best. They may not be where you are but they love you enough to want to see you be successful. They are supportive and believe in your goals as much as you do. They remind you of all the reasons you deserve to be a winner. These are the people you sit on the bed with to share your passions. You may even do all of this while eating ice cream and donuts as you binge watch your favorite Netflix series.

Your social counsel is also there to hold you accountable. They don't enable your self-pity. They call you on you bull. You may have several individuals who fit this category and that is fine. The more support networks you have the better.

Identify at least two (2) individuals that would fit into the social counsel category of your life?

1. _____

2. _____

Center S

The center S in the 3S model is self-counsel. The self-counsel is a constant. You can fire, demote or replace the others but you're stuck with yourself. If everyone else in your life disappears, you will still be there. The self-counsel category is a stand-alone category. Self-counsel is in the middle of the triangle because everything revolves around the self. There are going to be times when you need to be alone with the quiet of your own mind. You will need to evaluate yourself and speak into your own life. This is the time you use to evaluate your needs, set goals and learn to be one with yourself.

There are three individuals in this category: me, myself, and I. Me, myself, and I are the 3 individuals you will depend on the most. Me, myself and I equate to you as a whole person. As a winner you need to learn that there are times when clarity will only come to you when you are alone. As with anything, balance in your life is crucial to the development of the winner within. The times when you are in self-counsel will be when you make the adjustments.

Don't discount the importance of your alone time. Use the time to center yourself so that you can hear from God. This will be when He is able to speak to you. Allow yourself to go through the healing process and grow through it as well. Shed that shame and empty your cup of pain. This is the time you must be selfish with your healing. You must protect your growth with everything you have.

You should value your journey, and how far you've come. Because of all the work you've put into the process of developing the winner in you, you should be in a place of peace and wholeness. By now you should begin to feel comfortable with who you are becoming and where you are headed. You should appreciate and celebrate the winner within. Stay in this positive space, this is where you will maintain your winning mindset. Practice being kind and patient with yourself. Remind yourself just how important, worthy and special you are to the world.

Identify at least three (3) individuals that would fit into the self-counsel category in your life? (*hint* all three are found in you*)

1. _____

    (found in you)

2. _____

    (found in you)

3. _____

    (found in you)

The 3S model, is a triangle model that helps to keep the winner balanced. To continue to win, it will be necessary to have these individuals identified in your life. The 3S model highlights the value of balance. This model emphasizes the simple fact that a winner can't win alone. It is okay to seek help and guidance from others. It is also okay to speak up about the things you might need as you develop and maintain the winner in you.

Let's recap the following types of counsel.

Spiritual Counsel

Made up of individuals who speak into your life. They give you encouragement and feed the spiritual parts of you.

Secular Counsel

The secular counsel is your therapist, life coach and/or mentor. I'd say it would be a good idea to have all three individuals in this category but make sure you have at least one.

Social Counsel

Individuals you see as best friends, close friends or anyone with whom you share a bond with including your partner. These are the people you hang out with when you need a pick me up. They might be the other winners in your life with whom you've connected.

You may have one person who fits all three categories. A supportive team has many members. One person cannot be your everything and win themselves too. All the individuals in the counsel categories are helpers placed in your life to help you carry out your mission. It is crucial that you begin to identify these individuals and utilize them for the purpose they serve.

Once you identify these people it is possible that their true purpose is only known to you. That's okay. If you know who they are, that is all that matters. If you want to share with them what category, and in what capacity they serve, that's fine too. Make sure you put thought, and effort, into selecting the people who will serve as your counsel. This is a support team that you're building. You need to look at the lineup. Ask yourself about the characteristics they possess that caused you to select them.

Determine if you have enough players to handle all the plays you'd like to execute that require an assist. Be sure that these people can fill the role. You shouldn't pick your best friend, who also happens to be a therapist, as your therapist. It is a conflict of interest.

When picking your counsel, be true to you and what your needs are. Call on them, seeking their guidance and assistance, whenever necessary. Allow them to hold you accountable as you hold yourself responsible for the decisions you make and goals you set in your life.

Below are chapter summary questions for you to answer.

How confident do you feel about assembling your 3S support system?

_____
_____
_____
_____

While putting your support system in place, what are some of the potential barriers you may face, if any?

_____
_____
_____
_____

If you haven't already done so, have you ever thought about seeing a therapist? If not, what factors would prevent you making an appointment to begin your therapeutic experience?

_____
_____
_____
_____

What personality traits will help you with deciding who to select for the 3S model categories?

_____
_____
_____
_____

Identify any challenges you may face when it comes to being vulnerable and opening up to others in your support system.

_____
_____
_____
_____

What emotional, mental, or physical factors prevent you from reaching out to others, if any?

_____
_____
_____
_____

Chapter 14

The Victory Lap

Dedication, hard work plus patience

"Dedication" - Nipsey Hussle, Victory Lap The Album

You made it! You have begun the amazing journey of finding the true winner in you. Remember all the concepts presented in this guide. Know that there is a winner in you, that is yearning to be discovered and maintained. No matter what you've experienced in the past, you still can go forth in your life and soar. I encourage you to spread your wings and fly high.

The lessons I've learned as I traveled this journey have been such eye-opening experiences. It is my hope that you can have similar experiences on your own journey. Know that everything is not going to be easy. There will be some tough and challenging times. The winner in you can face any situation life throws at you.

Believe in your greatness and focus on your future. Your best is yet to come. I will be on the sideline cheering on every winner who is living their W.O.W. experience. The W.O.W. Effect is not just a thing that you do one time. The W.O.W. Effect is a movement, a lifestyle. You must intentionally work at maintaining the winner in you until it becomes automated.

Don't just read the book, live its lessons. Follow through, and follow up, will be essential. Don't allow yourself to become distracted from or lost along your winning journey. You've spent too many years wasting time, just going through the motions. You are at the point in your life where you need to get serious about what you want. Becoming a winner is not for the faint of heart. You need to come with your superhero mentality so that you can crush your goals. You need to W.O.W. as you grow into your winning mentality. Everything it takes to set a goal, execute the plans and win is already in you. You must stand on that fact and believe. Others can't believe it for you. Listen to God as He speaks life into your goals and dreams. Don't allow fear to paralyze or stunt your growth as a winner. Know that you have the power to control your destiny.

Share these tips and tools with others, and plant seeds of hope into the minds of future winners. Know that it is okay to seek out and ask for help or guidance. Know that doing so does not make you weak but shows how humble and strong you truly are.

Be a winner with integrity. Know that even when things don't go your way, you are still a winner because winners never quit. Remember that giving up is not an option. Every person who is a part of the W.O.W. movement is silently waiting for you to win. We're cheering you on. Life hasn't been easy, but you've made it this far. There is a winner inside of you, a hero inside waiting to be called into action. You must give yourself permission to manage your life so that they can lead you to your greatness.

The next level of winning is here. It is too late to turn around or become weary. You passed that exit when you decided to pick up this book. Below are your winner take-aways from each chapter. Use this as quick reference as needed.

Winner Take-A-Ways

Chapter 1: Mindset of A Winner

1. Winning is not a one-time event, it's something you do every day.
2. Prepare your mind to see the winner in you.
3. Winning is a mindset that is only developed over time.
4. You possess what it takes to win.
5. You must have clarity of what a winner looks like to you as defined on your own terms.

6. Be patient with yourself and expect the unexpected.

Chapter 2: The E.F.F.E.C.T. Model

1. The winner operates with a winning mentality.
2. The higher you climb, the less people will be at the top to meet you
3. You must see yourself moving from a place of fear and begin to stand in a place of faith.
4. No matter what you have gone through or what you may face, you must know that you can win.
5. Don't allow past mistakes to cloud your bright future.
6. At the root of every excuse is one of three things laziness, fear or lack of planning.

Chapter 3: Winning is a Choice

1. Deciding to win and operate with a winning mindset is a conscious choice.
2. Even in the face of adversity, a winner doesn't give up, they don't throw in the towel and surrender to the woes of life.
3. It takes someone strong, someone like you, to get up and face every day like a champ.
4. You might be making tiny moves, but at the end of the day, you are still choosing to move forward.
5. Surround yourself with likeminded people who encourage your progress and are as vested in your win as you are.

Chapter 4: Getting to the Root of the Issue: Doing the Work

1. Begin the process of identifying core issues that may prevent you from moving forward on your winning journey.

2. Defining who you are by looking in the mirror.
3. You are not on a stage every minute of your life, so your worth and self-acceptance don't need to come solely from the validation of others.
4. When we fail to resolve the core of our trust issues deeper issues may emerge in our relationships including depression, fear of rejection, feelings of unworthiness, or being unlovable.
5. Do what you need to do to heal you so that the real winner inside can finally stand up.

Chapter 5: Winners are Honest: Live Out Your Truth

1. Part of being honest with yourself is being honest with others.
2. Shift the areas in your life that need to be adjusted.
3. Acknowledge and taking accountability for the decisions you've made.
4. As you begin to speak, and live with your truths you are emotionally removing the shackles placed on you by others, real or imagined.

Chapter 6: Removing the Mask

1. Know who you are and do the work so that you're able to operate as a winner.
2. Be a maskless winner in a world full of impostors.
3. Facing who you truly are can be the scary side of becoming a winner.
4. Core issues are the inaccurate beliefs we have about ourselves. Take time to heal the core issues inside of you.
5. Never give up in your quest to better yourself.
6. Allow your light to shine because you've been dimming it for far too long.

Chapter 7: I am a Survivor

1. We minimize the effect our past experiences have on our present-day life by working through issues in order to remain authentic versions of ourselves.
2. Being a winner and overcoming is not just about surviving.
3. No matter how big or small, all winners have survived the past experiences of their lives.
4. You have survived 100% of your days, those are great odds that you will also live to survive today.
5. Winners keep going even in the face of adversity.
6. Winning is not always easy and there will be times when you want to give up, but as a winner, you won't give up (GIVING UP IS NOT AN OPTION).

Chapter 8: Learning to Let Go and Allowing God to Have Full Control

1. When you trust God, you trust that everything will be okay.
2. By trusting your God given intuition, listening to your gut, being faithful and relinquishing control to God is the way you become a successful winner.
3. Don't allow your shortcomings, or the mistakes you've made, to derail you from your destiny.
4. The winner is not focused on the problem but is more focused on the solution. As a winner trust yourself and your ability to trust God.

Chapter 9: Overcoming: The Rebirthing of a Winner

1. Some elevations in your life are going to require isolation. Learn to be okay being alone with yourself.

2. When it comes to boundaries, you must make sure that they are clearly defined and effectively communicated.
3. Winners don't give up, but they do take time to acknowledge their true feelings.
4. Winners are free to live in their truth, free to walk in their purpose, and free to forgive themselves for not loving themselves enough before.
5. When you begin to live and speak your truth, you have the power to be more successful and not just survive, but win.

Chapter 10: The Superhero vs. The Villain Within

1. As you begin to operate with a winning mindset, you need to see ourselves as a winner with the strength of a superhero.
2. Your inner hero motivates you to act.
3. Winners take equal responsibility for their successes and failures.
4. When a winner thinks about whining, they know the time has come to stop and evaluate.
5. Becoming a winner happens in three distinct steps of equal importance: overcome your whining; act on your wishes; maintain your winning streak. Winning is work.

Chapter 11: Setting Goals and Crushing Them

1. The first step to crushing your goals is to set them.
2. When setting your goals be sure to set reasonable timelines that are realistic.
3. Before you can execute your goal, you must evaluate its purpose in your life.
4. Winners are open, and willing, to putting the work in to get them to where they need to be.
5. It is important for you to believe in your own abilities to accomplish your goals.

6. Everyone is not going agree with all the goals you set for your life and know that, that is okay.

Chapter 12: The Evolution: Continuing the Process

1. As you develop the winner in you, you will have to evaluate your views of people and the world.
2. In order to elevate and go higher, you will need to leave some of the places that are comfortable.
3. Winners take a deep dive into their issues and resolve them.
4. Evolution is a continuous process that is aligned with maintaining the winner in you.
5. Get to a place where you can be at peace with fulfilling your purpose.
6. Take time to breath, relax and slow down. Life isn't a race.
7. Don't allow people to dictate how you get to feel and when you get to feel it.
8. Keep reminding yourself that you have the power to win.

Chapter 13: The Power to Seek Out, Access and Ask for Help

1. Use the 3s model to help keep you accountable while on your winning journey.
2. If what you are facing is too hard, know that it is ok to reach out and ask for help.
3. Every support system has their place in your life
4. With the help of the right therapist, the things you might be holding onto might be revealed and resolved.
5. Once you begin to heal yourself, some of the people around you will begin to look different.
6. Don't discount the importance of your alone time. Use the time to center yourself so that you can hear from God.

7. When picking your counsel, be true to you and what your needs are. Call on them and seek their guidance and assistance whenever necessary.

I thank you in advance for putting in the work and for elevating your life. Share your W.O.W. with others and inspire them to do the same. I have one final thing I need you to do before you finish this book. Right now, I need you to say out loud to yourself, 'I am a winner. I am the W.O.W. Effect in the flesh.' Say it one more time, 'I am a winner. I am the W.O.W. Effect in flesh.' That's it!

~Your W.O.W. is Now!

ABOUT THE AUTHOR

Cortina Peters is a licensed mental health counselor, life coach, author, motivational speaker and mentor who motivates people to win in every area of their life. She completed both her master's in mental health counseling and her bachelor's in psychology at Nova Southeastern University. Cortina started her career in the field of sexual health education and overall wellness over 20 years ago. She has been providing professional counseling services since 2009.

As the creative developer and visionary of the W.O.W. Effect, she bridges the gap between people just living life and those who are able to thrive and live life to the fullest. . She helps others become individuals who are able to experience life on the deepest level. She is a two-time cancer survivor and lupus warrior, she had dedicated her life to motivating, and encouraging, others to live their most authentic lives. She is an advocate for change and an activist in her own right. Having to fight for her life in ways many people wouldn't understand, she serves as a light to those who might be in dark, dull or dim places. Her bubbly, outgoing, personality makes it easy for anyone to connect with her. Her genuine commitment to seeing, and showing, people how to win is infectious. Her motto, iWin|iWon|iW.O.W., is something she encourages others to do as well.

For bookings and more information about programs visit:

www.iamcortinapeters.com

www.ingramcontent.com/pod-product-compliance
Lightning Source LLC
Chambersburg PA
CBHW071342080526
44587CB00017B/2930